24433

V94

A HISTORY OF EAST AFRICA

AN INTRODUCTORY SURVEY

BY

ZÖE MARSH

AND

G. W. KINGSNORTH

FOURTH EDITION OF
AN INTRODUCTION TO
THE HISTORY OF
EAST AFRICA

CAMBRIDGE
AT THE UNIVERSITY PRESS
1972

Published by the Syndics of the Cambridge University Press
Bentley House, 200 Euston Road, London NW1 2DB
American Branch: 32 East 57th Street, New York, N.Y.10022

Library of Congress Catalogue Card Number: 72–171677

ISBNS
0 521 08348 6 school
0 521 08346 x clothbound
0 521 09677 4 paperback

First published 1957
Second Edition 1961
Third Edition 1965

Typeset in Great Britain
by C. Tinling & Co. Ltd., London and Prescot
Printed in Nairobi by Kenya Litho Ltd.
Cardiff Road, Nairobi.

ACKNOWLEDGEMENTS

Thanks are due to the following for permission to reproduce photographs and maps: Fig 1 The Science Museum, London; Fig 2 Mrs M. C. Duyvendak; Figs 7 and 8 Kenya Information Services; Fig 9 Tanzania Information Services; Fig 10 The Grosvenor Gallery, London.

CONTENTS

PREFACE

In 1956, *An Introduction to the History of East Africa* was written in Nairobi and pioneered the study of East Africa as a whole, giving roughly equal weight to each territory. Advancing years bring changing perspectives, requiring adjustments of emphasis. Since the original form in which this book was published, in 1957, the four countries which make up East Africa have all attained independence; two have amalgamated. In addition, research has provided a clearer outline of events before the mid-nineteenth century and the significance of the colonial period can now be seen in a new perspective. Nations usually possess a distinctive culture; those in East Africa certainly do. A section on developments in art, music, and literature has therefore been added to the final chapter. In this version of the history of East Africa, therefore, greater emphasis has been placed on the pre-colonial period and the vital years after 1945. This makes it no longer possible to retain the familiar framework of the original book.

For most of us the words 'school text-book' have disagreeable associations, and it is hoped that the general reader will not be repelled by the fact that this book was primarily designed for students in connection with a school certificate syllabus. It was written with the hope also that the story of East Africa's growth would prove sufficiently interesting and readable to appeal to many others. But, because we were thinking especially of schools, emphasis has been laid on the biographical presentation of material and the content has been influenced by the amended history syllabus for school certificate candidates at centres in East Africa, which came into effect from January 1971.

We have worked closely together throughout the writing of the book and share responsibility for it equally. Authorship of particular chapters is as follows: by Z. M. 1, 2, 3, 4, 9, 10, 11, 12; by G. W. K., 5, 6, 7, 8.

Specialist checking and criticism of parts of the draft for the original publication in 1957 were most kindly given by Mr H. B. Thomas, O.B.E., Dame Margery Perham, D.C.M.G., Professor R. Oliver, Mr J. Moffett C.M.G., Miss D. Middleton, Mr J. Smart, M.B.E., D.P.A. and Sheikh Mubarak Ahmad. Similar help has been given in this version by Professor Beachey, former Professor of History at Makerere University College and now Professor of History at the University of Waterloo,

Ontario, and Dr Nicholls, author of *The Swahili Coast* (Allen and Unwin 1971). They are, of course, in no way responsible for any shortcomings that there may be, but we do feel very grateful to them.

April 1971   Z. M.
                                                    G. W. K.

MAPS

An area of major population movements

Chapter 1

EARLY HISTORY OF EAST AFRICA

PROLOGUE

The human revolution. In history we read about great changes in man's way of life. There were political, economic and scientific revolutions which began in America, Europe or Asia, but the fundamental revolution almost certainly began in Africa. Africa may have first produced the creature which we call man and so been the mother of mankind. The process of change was a slow one, and may have begun about 20–30 million years ago, when the primates who had been living in trees found that the forests were growing smaller, and they had to come down and live among the grass and other vegetation. As weak animals, they must have felt very unprotected from their enemies. When they wanted to find out where their enemies were they probably stood on their legs and looked over the long grass. An animal that walks on its hind legs is a biped. Its forelegs can develop the power to hold things and use them. Gradually these become hands with a thumb separate from the fingers. The first human bipeds we know about were the *Australopithecines*; and at Olduvai gorge, in Tanzania, Dr and Mrs Leakey unearthed a very fine skull of a biped, which they called *Zinjanthropus*, after the old name for the East African coast. Since then, fragments of ten others have been found at Olduvai, which is the most important stone-age site in the world.

The importance of the *Australopithecines* is that they knew how to make tools and used them regularly, with a definite purpose in mind: this is the accepted difference between men and the primates. The first tools were probably sharp stones which they found could be used for cutting or tearing, instead of relying on their big teeth. Soon they were looking round for these stones when they wanted to get some meat from a bone, or cut a branch off a tree for a spear. The next stage came when they found out how to break a stone to get a sharp edge and how to make use of the splintered edges of bones. At the same time these early men were beginning to live together in communities, which helped them to protect themselves. Taken together these two changes meant that Man was no longer entirely at the mercy of his environment. He had become adaptable, and began hunting instead of only scavenging. When his prey was the larger animals, he tried to use stone tools specially made for

1

killing and stunning. With his developing brain he could also now pass on a plan of action through language, and began to hunt in small groups of probably no more than thirty. Life for a woman was also changing. Her babies were born in a more immature state. This meant that she could take less part in hunting and had more time with her young, to whom she could pass on ideas; a home base was also needed. This was usually near a place where water was adequate and the animals Man hunted came to drink. He may also have done some fishing. These hunters and food gatherers appeared to find forests too difficult to live in. They sought open country, like the Eastern rift valley in East Africa and parts of the Transvaal in South Africa, which was relatively free from trees and thick bush. Olduvai was beside a lake in *Zinjanthropus*'s time, though now all the water has to be brought in a lorry. By 50,000 B.C. African man had found out how to use fire and to cook. He could also gum small flakes of stone on to wooden hafts to make barbs, which would ensure that a wounded animal left a clear trail of blood to follow. These barbs might also be smeared with poison. By now the first period of the stone age in East Africa was nearly over; it lasted down to 50,000 B.C. and was followed by a middle period, which continued until about 10,000 B.C., and a final one, which in some parts did not end till about 1400 A.D.

By the beginning of the last period of the stone age, hunting groups had begun to move into the other continents, but Africa was probably still the most densely populated of the continents, with about 3–4 million inhabitants (in 1970 there were about 280 million). By the end of the middle period, a new people with thinner, longer bones had reached East Africa, who must have looked rather like men from North Africa or South-West Africa. They brought new techniques in using stone, made pottery and beads and may have had bows and arrows. Man was now able to live in less open country, and we have evidence of sites in the thickly-wooded parts of western Uganda. Some men were beginning to live in settled communities. These people often buried their dead, instead of leaving them to be eaten by scavenging animals, so we can find out more about the way of life of these people, the sites of whose living-quarters are often found under overhanging rocks or in caves.

In Gamble's cave, Elmenteita, the skeletons are of men over 5 foot 10 inches, covered with ochre, possibly to represent blood. It looks as if they had enough leisure to make bowls and decorate themselves with ochre and beads. Other sites, used by fishermen, have been found near Lakes Rudolf and Edward, where they may have paddled out in boats. There is a particularly interesting site near Lake Nakuru, called the

Njoro River cave, where about eighty people were cremated, each with a pestle and mortar and a stone bowl beside them, which could have been used for cooking. These tools were also probably used for grinding the corn they were beginning to grow now that they were settling down. Like the people in Gamble's cave, they were also fond of decorating themselves with beads – to judge from the large number found. These included five complete necklaces, one $27\frac{1}{2}$ inches (69 centimetres) long and probably worn as a double string.

A good deal of what we know about the life of early man comes from his paintings on the walls and ceilings of overhanging rocks where he sheltered. Flat surfaces made a good canvas, and the colours came from the earth; ochre, for instance, could be ground down to produce yellow, brown and red; charcoal or manganese gave black; white came from kaolin or guano. (Green or blue, if they were used, have not lasted, which is not surprising as they would have had to be made from vegetable dyes.) Fingers, feathers or twigs would be the brushes used by these able artists, whose favourite subjects were the animals they hunted, usually buck, giraffe, elephant and buffalos, which they enjoyed eating, and whose skins, stitched together with needles made from bones, they could use for clothing. Some think that they painted animals to bring luck in the next day's hunting. They needed it, for most animals were much bigger than they are today; sheep, for instance, looked like buffalos with giant horns, sometimes 12 foot wide. There are a number of these rock paintings near Kondoa in Tanzania and some of them include people. At Kolo, for instance, there is a painting of two men holding a woman whom two others are trying to drag away.

From around 500 A.D., the use of iron was introduced into East Africa, and the hunting and food-gathering peoples slowly began to disappear. A few, however, are still to be found in Karamoja, and in Kenya a hunting people, called the Dorobo, were still fairly common at the end of the nineteenth century. The iron age came to an end in East Africa about 1800 B.C. Written records, and here and there careful study of oral traditions, combined with archaeology, are allowing a picture of life at that period to emerge; but it must be remembered that, apart from the coast, East Africa was isolated, and even trade goods never reached most parts till about the seventeenth century A.D.

Before continuing the story of the iron age in East Africa, a brief note of caution must be added. The evidence which is being pieced together varies in its reliability, and there are still large gaps in our knowledge. Archaeology can fill some of these, but our description of society in the interior of East Africa, prior to the middle of the nineteenth century, still depends largely on oral traditions – family records storing up the names of a man's ancestors back to the sixteenth century testify to the length of old women's memories. Traces of eucalyptus hedges may supplement the tradition of an earlier settlement of huts. Songs, ceremonies and place-names may provide clues. This material has to be examined cautiously; stories, for example, may be true of the people who tell them, but refer to some other place from which they have moved. Help can sometimes be obtained from studying the language people speak, social anthropology and such techniques as radio-carbon dating. Unfortunately East Africa is a difficult area for the archaeologist. He is handicapped in places by dense vegetation, and finds that the acid soils destroy human remains and are mostly too shallow to hold traces of the flimsy homes of migrant communities. Considerable help can, however, be obtained by examining the environment which gave rise to the movements of the early people. Perhaps 'peoples' is not quite the right word; one suggestion is that the word 'population' might be better, indicating large movements, under large influences over long periods, of numerous peoples, who were unlikely ever to be aware of one another's existence.

The environment. The East African environment was, and is, a harsh one. Difficult features are: insufficient rainfall; light, easily-exhausted soils; prevalence of tsetse-fly; and the lack of material resources. 30 inches (75 centimetres) of rainfall is usually regarded as being needed for intensive arable cultivation; less than that, i.e. 20 inches (50 centi-metres), makes ranching possible. Yet in 4 out of 5 years only 20 per cent of East Africa obtains between 30 and 20 inches; moreover, nearly two-thirds of the area has an annual drought for 6 months. Kenya is the least fortunate country; 72 per cent usually gets less than 20 inches of rainfall a year; for Uganda the figure is 13 per cent and for Tanganyika 16 per cent.

Pastoral development is further handicapped by the widespread prevalence of the tsetse-fly which not only carries sleeping-sickness to humans, but also spreads *ngana* to animals, and largely accounts for the lack of transport other than human porterage until the end of the nineteenth century. An examination of Map 1 shows that Kenya is the least-infested area in the present day, and Tanganyika the most. Comparison of rainfall on this map with Map 2, showing relief, will suggest desirable areas of settlement for agriculturalists and pastoralists. But it is a mistake to assume a rigid division between these. Very few peoples fall exclusively into one group or the other; even the Maasai find that their grassland cannot maintain all who speak their language. Some

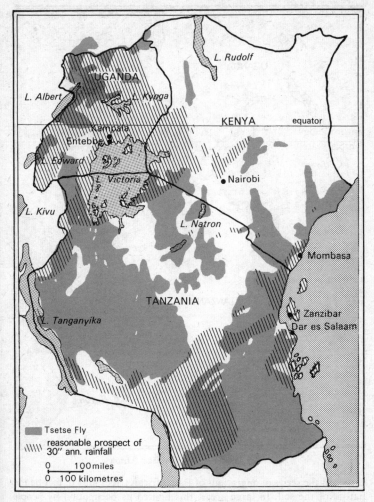

Map 1 The distribution of tsetse-fly and rainfall in East Africa (based on a map by Director of Colonial Surveys)

have to eke out the traditional diet of milk and blood with grain foods, and the Arusha Maasai rely on intensive agriculture. Study of the soil reveals it to be light and easily exhausted, and helps explain the custom of shifting cultivation in order to 'rest' it. Vegetation is unevenly distributed and in some parts of the country there is an excessive tropical growth, while in others there are semi-desert conditions. One of the

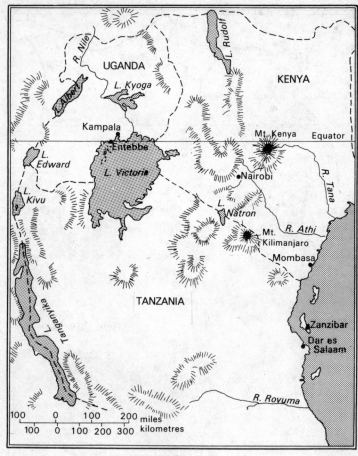

Map 2   A relief map of East Africa

causes of the series of migrations of East African tribes may in fact be the nature of the soil. In large areas, this limited its occupation by people without modern agricultural knowledge. The environment also helps to explain the present distribution of the population, which is thinly spread over an area of 642,728 square miles of land. Large parts of East Africa are semi-desert, and in addition there are 38,901 square miles of water, though there are pockets of considerable density of population. Of this compact block Kenya occupies 219,789 square miles of land, giving her (according to the 1969 census-figure of 10,890,000 inhabitants) a density of 42 inhabitants to a square mile of land, compared to approximately 60 taking the world as a whole. Even today, therefore, East Africa has comparatively few people to the square mile; and there are good reasons to think that there were even fewer at the end of the nineteenth century. This may well have been due not only to disease but also to the slave-trade, and the wars between tribes that often went with it. African society evolved to meet human needs within this environment, in which the mere existence of an individual depended on his relationship to the whole community. So long as he remained within it, he was sure of protection and assistance in time of need.

The Bantu. By about 1300 A.D. a negroid population, speaking Bantu languages, had spread into the heavy rainfall areas, leaving the drier plains and grasslands to the pastoralists who followed them, and driving the food-gatherers and hunters up into the colder, higher forests or the more arid plains. Here and there, their survivors can be found today, the pygmies of Uganda, for instance, and the Dorobo of Kenya. Although cattle were a source of wealth to the Bantu, and many of them had large herds, they were basically an agricultural people who lived in small, relatively-settled communities. They also appear to have combined belief in a supreme being (whose concern with mankind is sometimes limited) with a close attachment to the spirits of their ancestors. The chief link between the Bantu people, however, is language. While they speak several hundred languages, these are all closely related. In all Bantu languages, for instance, the use of the suffix and prefix is similar and has an important effect on the meaning of the word. Their origin is still uncertain, although there is some evidence that Bantu speech may have developed in the area around the Congo–Zambezi watershed and spread through East Africa from the interlacustrine area (between the lakes: see Map p. vi), probably reaching the coast more than 1,000 years ago. Meanwhile there were invasions of the country by Cushite populations. Today the majority of the people of East Africa are the descendants, in varying proportions, of Cushites, Bushmen and Negroes.

Ironworking and agricultural development. It is probable that in the early years of the iron age, which, it has been suggested, began about 1000 A.D., there was a sudden increase in population among the Bantu. This could have been triggered off by the use of iron, and the intro-duction of the banana and the yam. Some writers think these innovations spread from the coast via the mouth of the Zambezi and the Great Lakes.

East Africa has more different kinds of bananas than anywhere else in the world and they provide the basic food of many Baganda today. But

Fig. 1   How iron used to be smelted in the iron age – a photograph of
          a reconstruction

bananas have to be grown from suckers and cannot be raised from seeds,
so the Bantu, who used them as a major source of food, must have given
up wandering and begun to settle, probably in a humid but not too
densely-forested area. To clear the land iron tools would have been
needed and the combination of new crops and the use of better tools
enabled a larger population to be supported.

Unfortunately there is insufficient archaeological evidence to enable
us to trace the route by which a knowledge of ironworking reached East
Africa. It could have been from Meroe, which was the centre of a
flourishing iron industry in the fourth century B.C., from Indonesia via

the Indian Ocean, from the south-west, or from all three. For the most part all the archaeological evidence we have to go on in East Africa is the remains of slag and bellow pipes; but the use in recent times in East Africa of bellows with a bowl furnace suggests that knowledge may have spread from Meroe via the Sudan.

At first knowledge of the craft seems to have been restricted to the Banyole and the Wasima who live on the north-eastern shore of Victoria Nyanza, but the high prices charged were an incentive to others to learn the skill. The Bukusu for instance at one time bought from the Wasima, and had to give a cow in exchange for a spear until they found out how to make spears themselves. Less fortunate tribes who had no iron ore in their land might have had to get their iron goods from a considerable distance. As Oliver points out, 'The frequency of the spear and hoe among the insignia of African chieftainship is a potent witness to the political significance of the blacksmith's art.' Even in the twentieth century Bantu iron smelters surround their craft with an air of mystery, and often have their furnaces some distance from settlements, so it is not easy to build up a picture of the process. There is, however, a promising site of early ironworking at Engaruka, about 20 miles south of Lake Natron, in Northern Tanzania. This is being excavated, and may yield some interesting information. Engaruka appears to have been the centre, for a thousand years, of an important agricultural settlement, and to have had a population of hundreds.

Migrations of the Nilotes. Although the Nilo-Hamitic and Nilotic peoples share a negroid ancestry with the Bantu people, their early history is different. As we have seen, the latter probably moved into the area from the west, south-west and south, and were already established in the fifteenth century when the first migrants moved down from Ethiopia in the north. These were the almost legendary Chwezi, who were the ancestors of the Watusi in Ruanda and Urundi. They were a pastoral people with chiefs, but their outstanding characteristic was their devotion to their long-horned cattle. In the kingdoms they established there was always one ruler with clearly-defined functions, but these were concerned with his immense herds of cattle rather than people. The king had the right to levy a tax of cows on the larger herds, and the lesser chiefs under him were mainly concerned with the care of the royal herds and settling disputes between herdsmen. There were no boundaries, for the only interest the land had for the chief and his followers was as pasture. The Bantu were, therefore, left free to cultivate it as they wished, and Bantu and Chwezi mingled together to form a loose confederation known as Kitara (the present day Bunyoro) of which a main centre was at Bigo, where great ditches have been found cut deep into the rock.

This confederation contained in it the seed of the concept of Uganda as a unit, which was further developed when the Luo Babito succeeded the Chwezi as rulers and forced the Hima (the name by which the Chwezi are usually known as they emerge more clearly from the mists of time) to withdraw into Ankole, Karagwe and Ruanda. About the sixteenth century, when the Portuguese had moved into the coast, the Hima expanded south to Sukumaland and from there to Nyamwezi country. Wherever they went the Bahima took with them their long-horned cattle and their system of chiefs, and in most regions appear to have been assimilated by the agriculturalists, who probably found the cattle-manure useful and the chiefs impartial judges in quarrels between members of different clans.

The Babito Nilotes. In Kitara the arrival of the Luo-speaking Nilotes about 1500 A.D. meant the displacement of the Chwezi dynasty by the Babito. The new rulers of Kitara, or Bunyoro as it is now known, were so few in number that they were assimilated by the Bantu over whom they ruled, and gave up their own language. They introduced, however, a more developed form of kingship, combining the functions of priest and king and showing as much concern with their subjects as with their cattle. Moreover, they had the advantage of ruling a people who were increasingly becoming agriculturalists; among agriculturalists difficulties can be settled without recourse to the frustrating blood-feud. Although cattle were not the obsession with the Babito that they had been with the Chwezi, the explorer Speke comments on a visit to Bunyoro, in 1863, 'The king's cows even are kept in his palace enclosure, the calves actually entering the hut, where like a farmer, Kumrasi (the Mukama of Bunyoro) walks amongst them.' Milk was still a major part of their diet; the skins of cattle provided the shields, bags, bedding, etc. that they used; and when they married the bride-price was paid in the cattle that provided fines and compensation for injury. Men even had nicknames based on their favourite cows.

But looking after cattle did not satisfy these people as it had the Chwezi; about the time of the seventeenth century, groups of warriors set out from Bunyoro on cattle-raids, claiming new lands for the Mukana of Bunyoro, who became the centre of a loosely-knit empire over which he ruled as a priest–king who personified his people. Until the nineteenth century, the history of Uganda is dominated by the history of Bunyoro and its related states of Buganda, Kohi, Kiziba, Toro and northern Busoga. The Kenyan historian, Dr Ogot, comments further, 'When the

British took over in 1894, Uganda, unlike Kenya, was not simply a geographical expression. Several attempts, some more successful than others, had been made to administer the whole area as a unit. In all these attempts the Nilotic factor was important. The Babito had consolidated the overlordship first established by the Chwezi.'

Nilotic migrations. The period before 1800 was characterised by mass migrations throughout the area which have few parallels elsewhere. These resulted in the interchange of ideas and skills, which led to the evolution of progressively larger and more complex societies. Most societies in East Africa have their origins in the large movements of populations which took place between the fifteenth and nineteenth century. (Thanks to Professor Ogot's research those of the Luo are known in detail.

This has already been shown in the case of Bunyoro. Parallel changes in response to new conditions have been traced in the history of the Nilotic people. These have the added interest of showing three different stages in settlement, which are therefore given in detail. In the first stage, they moved into occupied territory. In the second stage, they were the first to clear the land; in the third stage, wars of conquest and a pattern of chiefs began to emerge. Three other case-histories have been selected to show the responses to new conditions made by:

(a) Agriculturalists – the Eastern Bantu;
(b) pastoralists – the Maasai;
(c) an agricultural chiefdom – the Chagga.

Other examples could have been taken.

During the fifteenth century the Nilotic people, who today number about $3\frac{1}{2}$ million, left their centre in the south-east part of the present Republic of the Sudan, searching for new pastures to relieve the pressure on their herds and people of overcrowding. They were looking for lowland country resembling the dry plains they had left behind, and at first skirted the steeper uplands like those round Kericho and high-rainfall areas like those near Kisumu; but pressure of numbers eventually forced them to occupy less attractive country. The Nuer and the Dinka moved north into almost unoccupied country and were followed by the Shilluk, and reference has already been made to the epoch-making group who moved into south-west Uganda and later fanned out from Bunyoro into Buganda. During the sixteenth century, the Luo were also moving steadily up the Nile Valley towards a destination in the area now usually called Chope. They seem then to have moved further north to Acholi, westwards into Alur and eastwards into Lango country; and so passed on to the north-east corner of Lake Victoria. As time passed, their environment forced further changes on the Luo. In the fertile land on the south-west of Victoria Nyanza, the branch now known as the Haya, they settled down to grow groves of bananas which provided them with food and beer. Along the north-east shores of the lake, further to the east, the Luo way of life was increasingly modified by their environment and became more and more like that of their Bantu neighbours, the Luyia. With these changes went a new love of the land; before that, their existence had been a semi-nomadic one, dominated by their cattle, in which no one piece of land was more precious than another. As Ogot writes, 'A man would readily leave his father's grave and build a new home several miles away, if the land in the latter place was better and enemies fewer.' The approximate date of the arrival of the Jok, the ruling class of the early Luo migrants, was between 1450 and 1550.

Settlement in Padhola. Early movements of the Luo people had been into occupied territories, but between about 1625 and the end of the century (probably due to pressure of population) the second stage began, and advance parties moved into Padhola, or West Budama, as it is called today. This was land that man had not tamed, and stories told of the settlement stress exciting fights with elephants and the hard work and hazards involved in controlling the forest. This was the promised land, one which, 'it seems God himself had specially isolated and preserved'. It was therefore a holy land in which each clan had a shrine and all shared in the development; finally Padhola evolved the cult of Bura. As all the clans took part in the clearing of the land, it did not become the exclusive possession of any of them and claims were based on first occupation; moreover, as the land had not been fought for no chieftainship grew up to parallel the development of Ntemi chiefdoms in the western half of modern Tanzania.

On their way to the promised land some of the clans gathered forces as they went, as the song says:

> We people of the Oruwa Dibworo we are quick to take.
> We meet a stranger, and very soon he becomes a Ja-Oruwa of
> Dibworo who comes along with us.

Others attracted the attention of the Banyole, whom they passed, by paying their way with iron goods, spears, axes, etc. As the Banyole also liked the useful wooden articles they made, they used to visit on a friendly basis, and relations between the Luo and Banyole only became strained as more and more of the latter pushed into Padhola; the real difficulty was that the area was a corridor without defensive sites.

By the mid-eighteenth century the old song

Eee.one child is not enough,
One child is inadequate,
Eee, when the war drum sounds 'tindi!'
Who will come to your rescue – one child!

was no longer relevant. By now almost without exception all the Luo clans had arrived, and with the coming of the Iteso, some two or three generations ago, the old migration corridor was filled in. The next problem came when the Teso families began to outnumber the Padhola in East Budama, which they now began to look on as their own. An offshoot of these Padhola then probably moved to Nyanza.

The third stage of Luo migration, and the settlement of western Kenya.
In Kenya, the first Luo arrivals faced a different set of problems from those which had confronted the early migrants into Padhola; Nyanza was an area which had been inhabited since the stone age, and was occupied by iron-using people at the time when the Saxon kings were ruling in England. It seems likely that by 1600 the first wave of Luo invaders, probably made up of large family groups of wandering pastoralists looking for a good water-supply and promising pastures for their flocks, had arrived, but we know no details of their lives. Finally, a small group appears to have settled on a hill named after a semi-mythical ancestor called Ramogi, and begun to till the ground as agriculturalists. The area in which they had settled consisted of a wide expanse of savannah country, with good access to water for cattle: to the east lay the River Yala and Lakes Kangabobi, Manbogo and Saur, which were easy to reach. This isolated area satisfied the newcomers till about the middle of the seventeenth century, and then they began to spread out into central Nyanza; expansion involved wars of conquest, and land was now occupied on that basis. Under the impact of war a pattern of chiefs began to emerge which by 1900 was clearly defined.

The final chapter was written when the Luo moved into South Nyanza; in its early stages this story presents a complex picture, the fragments of which are still being pieced together. It is clear, however, that the Luo were not the only people on the move in this area. The Gusii were drifting from the Kano plains by the shore of Victoria Nyanza, along the line of the present railway, which runs from Kisumu eastwards. Eventually they were brought up against a Kipsigis settlement at Lumbwa, which turned them towards Kericho; here famine twisted their route south-westwards.

Between Lake Kyoga and Victoria Nyanza there is a corridor which links Uganda and Nyanza, and sometime between 1780 and 1820 the Abajunta forced their way from Buganda into Nyanza. The story goes that this move was the result of a ruthless attack by the kabaka, Junju, on the wife of his brother and successor, Semakorkiro. Acting on the advice of the queen mother, Semakorkiro moved his forces away until they were ready to attack the kabaka. But Semakorkiro seems to have considered an attack on royalty, even at his own command, as a dangerous precedent; and when the kabaka was killed by followers, led by Kiboye, he secretly arranged to have the followers themselves massacred at a feast. Details of the plan, however, leaked out in time for them to fly east and west; a group led by Kiboye escaped from Kampala in a boat, finally settling on one of the islands in Victoria Nyanza, and from there expanded into southern Nyanza.

Luo migration southwards was finally halted by the coming of the Germans and the British. Northwards and eastwards it was checked by geographical factors. Moreover, the Luo were contained by pressure from other nomad people, the Nandi and the Teso for example. With the British declaration of a protectorate over Kenya, in 1895, large-scale movements were at an end, and the shifting boundaries were about to be frozen. But before leaving the story of the settlement of western Kenya, some reference must be made to the Luyia. By the seventeenth century their ancestors had shifted first from eastern Uganda to central Nyanza as it is called today and from there to southern Buluyia. The last move in the settlement came when pressure built up in eastern Uganda, which had been invaded by the Teso, who forced many of the inhabitants into northern Buluyia.

The Eastern Bantu (*agriculturalists*). Today the Bantu in Kenya and Uganda are to be found in three areas. Reference has already been made to the first two, that is, the lake regions of western Uganda and western Kenya; the third is in eastern Kenya, where pressure from the Galla and Somali may have been one reason why the Embu, Kikuyu, Kamba and Meru moved inland from the Shungwaya area on the coast; another may have been increasing drought. In the Meru language the word for north also means right, and the word for south, left; west is *ruguru* which also means upwards. Now the Meru have a tradition that they moved to their present land from the coast upwards, or *ruguru*, to the highlands inland: in doing so the north would be on their right. Their traditions are further supported by finding the sites of abandoned villages to the east, i.e. the start of their route, but not to the west, nearing the end of the journey. It has also been suggested that the Embu moved up the River Tana from the coast and settled inland about 1425, and that earlier still the Kamba had travelled up the Athi river to their present site. According to this reconstruction of the past, the Kikuyu must have reached the Fort Hall area about 1545, and moved on to Kiambu about 1800. Age-sets and traditional generations have been used for working out these dates, but the outline is still shadowy.

Pastoral migrations – the Maasai. We know few details of the past of the Nilo-Hamitic peoples, who include the Nandi, Kalenjin, Iteso and the Maasai, but it would appear that they entered Kenya near Kapoeta, north of Lake Rudolf. The first of the peoples to move south were the Kalenjin. In the early seventeenth century, the Nandi moved along the Nandi escarpment, expanding northwards. Soon they were involved in struggles to the north and east with the Maasai, who travelled south passing Lake Rudolf on the east and overtaking the Nandi.

Among the Maasai, there are legends of an ancestor called Maasinda, who made a great ladder to help them climb up from Lake Rudolf to the Uasin Gishu plateau, north of Kitale. Tradition says that they then spread over the central part of the Kenya Highlands, possibly at the end of the sixteenth century, and south down the Rift Valley into Tanganyika. The Maasai were travelling down a passage of pasture-land, good for cattle but not much use to cultivators, and were only finally halted by the Hehe, about 1830. As a result of this, the Barugya section of the tribe gave up pastoral pursuits and began to cultivate the soil. Eventually they joined the Taveta on the south-eastern slopes of Mount Kilimanjaro. Another group turned northwards again and pushed through Kikuyuland to the rich grazing-land of Laikipia. From their bases the Maasai warriors raided far and wide – a distance of 300 miles was no obstacle; but even the Maasai were checked by steep slopes and thick forests, and the Kamba, the Taita, the Meru, the Kikuyu, and others who were fortunate in their natural sanctuaries, all survived.

Eastern Bantu migrations to Chaggaland. The great snow-capped peak of Kilimanjaro looks as if it is floating above the clouds, which sometimes cut it off from view altogether. It serves as a huge signpost in the sky to those in the Kamba hills in the north, and beyond them to the Kikuyu. It can be seen by the Taita and the Taveta and is usually visible from the plains on the south and west. It is a familiar sight to the Maasai who graze their cattle there. It is not surprising that the Chagga people have a very strong sense of place and that the mountain is the focus of their history for, apart from its magnetism, it is an oasis of water, food and pasture in a dry, open plain. The account that follows is based on *A History of the Chagga People on Kilimanjaro*, which was written at the request of the Chaggaland Trust.

According to the oral traditions of the Sambaa, Pare and Chagga people, Kilimanjaro, the Pare Mountains and the Suambara were unpopulated till about 1500, and it was not until the eighteenth century that there was a migration into the area. The base of Kilimanjaro is surrounded by forest, which starts at about 6,000 feet and extends upwards for 1,500 to 3,000 feet. Above this is savannah country, through which migrants passed before drifting downwards to settle in the fertile lower region below the forest. Others preferred to stay in the high plateau-land, where they could hide their cattle in the forest if attacked. Innumerable tracks lead up the steep ravines, but three main routes have always been used; an upper track rising through the forest and circling the high plateau of Shira, which lies between the peaks Kibo and Mawenzi, a middle track passing through the most populous part and a lower track following the plain at the base. Even today a good deal of Chaggaland is very imperfectly known, but evidence suggests that the original migrants came mostly from the north-east, certainly during the period when the Galla were pressing down from the north. There may well have been movements also from the south of peoples driving others north and there appear to have been two important centres from which newcomers spread out. The first of these, to which reference was made above, is the high plateau that stretches above the forest between the two peaks Kibo and Mawenzi. Here the chiefs of Siha established themselves.

Further to the east the Kikafu basin formed a dispersal centre for those who came up from the plain and spread out over the fertile land enclosed in its fan-like system of streams. The Kikafu basin seems to have been a dispersal centre also for Mount Meru, some 25 miles to the south-west of Kilimanjaro, and this may account for the similarity in law and customs between the peoples of these two areas. Two or three waves of migrants seem to have moved from one to the other. Those who settled in the Kikafu basin claim Machame as an ancestor, and he has given his name to the chiefdom. Coming meanwhile from the west, and moving eastwards, were the Orio clan, who are the royal chiefly clan of Kibosho. They had come from the west, moved eastwards by the upper track above the forest, carrying iron spears and driving many cattle, and paused near the lands of Reguna, chief of the Machame. Here their young men were playing before initiation rites when they were all slaughtered by the Machame on the orders of Reguna, who later claimed to rule half Kilimanjaro. Demoralised by this shocking attack, the Orio clan later moved further to the east and joined their fellow Kibosho, who had already settled in the fertile middle zone of Chaggaland, which lay near the caravan routes to Mombasa in the north and Pangani in the south. The last of the chiefdoms to be settled may well have been that of Moshi, which produced Mangi Rindi, an outstanding diplomat who impressed his personality on travellers, missionaries and German officials.

CHAPTER 2

KILWA AND THE COASTAL STATES

External contacts. Although East Africa has not been an easy place to reach by land, it is not so inaccessible by sea. Before the Suez Canal was cut, the shortest sea-route from Europe to East Africa was over 8,000 miles. By contrast, the distance from Zanzibar to Bombay is only 2,500 miles (about the length of the Mediterranean Sea). Therefore, while early visitors to West Africa came mostly from Europe, those to East Africa came from Asia. These visitors to East Africa were helped by the fortunate direction of the monsoon winds, which start to blow from the north-east in December and from the south-west in March. Very early on, the Arabs realised that this meant that their dhows could be blown south to East Africa by the monsoon in December, and, a few months later, driven back by the same wind, when it had changed direction. The dhows were similar to those which today still use the monsoons to sail up and down the east coast of Africa. Most of the places mentioned in this chapter can be found on map 3.

Greek ships probably first sailed to the south round Cape Guardafui searching for ivory in the time of Ptolemy III, who reigned in Egypt from 247–221 B.C. In A.D. 45 a Roman sailor, Hippalus, noticed the regularity of the monsoon winds. The knowledge soon spread; books were written in Greek and Latin telling of the Indian Ocean and its ports. One of these books was a guide-book to the Indian Ocean. Its title was *Periplus* (circumnavigation or sailing round) *of the Erythraean Sea*, as the Greeks and Romans called the Indian Ocean. This book still exists today, and in it we find references to East Africa, where there lived along the coast 'men of piratical habits, very great in stature, and under separate chiefs for each place'. To the coast there came 'Arab captains and agents, who are familiar with the natives and intermarry with them and who know the whole coast and understand the language. There are imported into these markets the lances made at Muza especially for this trade, and hatchets and daggers and awls, and various kinds of glass.' The *Periplus* tells us that the Arabs also imported a little wheat, not so much for trading purposes as to secure the goodwill of the native inhabitants of the coast, for 'there are exported from these places a great quantity of ivory ... and rhinoceros horn and tortoiseshell ... and a little palm oil'; while from just below Cape Guardafui there were

17

exported 'slaves of the better sort which are brought to Egypt in increasing numbers'.

At some time between the late fourth and early fifth century A.D., direct contact between the Mediterranean and the Indian Ocean stopped. Very little is recorded about the period from then until the late seventh century. After that, contemporary Arab geographers provide an outline of the history of the east coast, from the tenth to the thirteenth century, from which we gather that it remained a largely non-Islamic, Negro area.

By the tenth century, Arab dhows were trading regularly with China, but the Chinese still regarded trade as something inferior. They liked to think of the foreigners from overseas as 'barbarians', bringing tribute to the emperor of China, after which they were allowed to trade. The more foreigners who came, the greater was the glory of the emperor. So in the fifteenth century A.D. a series of expeditions was sent overseas to bring back the luxuries which the Chinese court enjoyed. The fifth of these expeditions went to Kenya, because of a giraffe which had been presented to the emperor. (The emperor had regarded it as a very good omen and seen that the ambassadors who brought it were escorted back to their home in Malindi.)

Early trade. All these visitors came for the sake of trade. They hoped to get from East Africa spices, ivory, skins and slaves, for which they would usually trade beads and cloth. In those days, spices were valued as preservatives, as well as for the flavour they gave to food, and they were obtained from the area round Cape Guardafui. Africa has always been the chief source of ivory, because its elephants are not used for work and are, therefore, hunted for their tusks. Unfortunately, Africa was also for centuries the centre of the slave-trade, and one of the centres for distribution was the East Africa coast, where trade caused town life to develop. In the towns the influence of Arab, Indian and Persian traders may have spread the Muslim faith. At any rate, when the traveller Ibn Battuta revisited the coast in 1331 he felt that he was among fellow-Muslims. By the fifteenth century, there were thirty-seven towns along the coastal strip between Kilwa and Mogadishu, and on the eve of the Portuguese voyages round the Cape of Good Hope to the Far East these towns were still prosperous.

Decline in Arab trade. From earliest times southern Arabia was the market for goods from the east, and the north-eastern monsoon brought Arabian dhows to the coast of East Africa. In the second century A.D., this trade decreased. First, the irrigation of south-west Arabia was seriously disturbed by the bursting of a large reservoir, which reduced

Fig. 2   The presentation of a giraffe from Africa to the emperor of China – picture from a Chinese manuscript

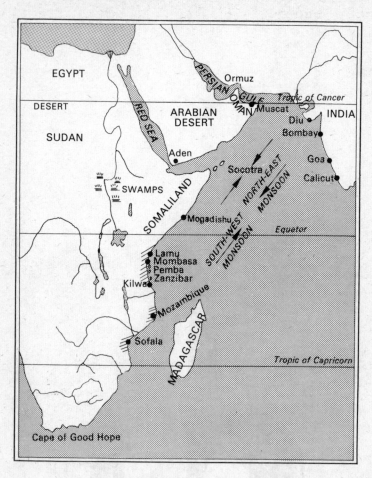

Map 3   The Indian Ocean in late fifteenth century

the prosperity of the whole of the area. Secondly, the Bantu people had begun to appear on the coast and, as they were fiercer and better armed than the original peoples, the Arab traders were further discouraged. Trade revived with the rise of Islam, and the arrival of Arab settlers on the coast. By the thirteenth century, Kilwa had control of the gold-trade from Sofala to the north and had contacts with the interior that may even have stretched as far as the Mali Empire, on the west coast.

Mohammed. Written records of coastal history are rare. Before the coming of the Portuguese much is, therefore, only guesswork. The first recorded happening stems from an event of great importance in the history of civilisation. This was the birth of Mohammed, in Mecca, in A.D. 570. He taught the Arabs to turn from heathen gods to the worship of one God. 'There is one God (Allah), and Mohammed is his Prophet.' Mohammed's teaching angered the rulers of Mecca, and in 622 he was forced to flee to Medina. His power and influence, however, continued to spread, and eight years later he was able to conquer Mecca. When Mohammed died in 638, practically the whole of Arabia had accepted the faith of Islam.

Impact of Islam. The chief political effect of Islam was that it united the tribes of Arabia, who were now determined to use their strength to convert as many people as possible to their new religion of *Islam,* which was the word they used for submission to the will of Allah. The Muslims believed that those who died fighting for their religion went straight to paradise, and they fought bravely and with strict discipline. In the first eighty years after the death of the Prophet they conquered Syria, Mesopotamia, Persia, and Egypt, and spread their empire through North Africa as far as Spain. At the head of this empire was the caliph (or successor) of the Prophet, and it was not long before disputes broke out as to who was the rightful caliph. These disputes divided the Arab Empire, and caused some of those who had been on the losing side to take refuge on the pleasant coast of East Africa, with which trade had already made them familiar.

A really reliable account of events affecting the East African coast from the seventh to the tenth century has not yet been found; various stories have come down to us, but whether they are true is not known; one such story follows. Among those who knew the coast well were the traders of Oman. Their land is in the north-east corner of Arabia and juts out into the Indian Ocean, with the Arabian desert behind it. Those who lived in Oman were, therefore, in a very good position for trade, and were quick to seize any chance to win independence. Among the lovers of independence were Suleiman and Said, who led a rebellion against the caliph towards the end of the seventh century A.D. When this failed, they had to flee to Zenjibar, or the 'land of the blacks' (*zenj* is a Persian word for black, and *bar* means coast). Two other groups of refugees followed: the people of Zaid, who left the Yemen because they hated the caliph, and the 'Seven Brothers' of El Hasa. The Seven Brothers were probably the seven leaders of a large group of warriors who left El Hasa, which at that time was the capital of a state in southern Mesopotamia. They conquered the whole coastal strip, down as far as Mombasa. Finally, Hasan bin Ali and his six sons set sail from southern Persia in seven ships, and each shipload founded a settlement. Four of these settlements are known: Mombasa, Pemba, Johanna in the Comoro Isles, and Kilwa. It was at Kilwa, which was already inhabited, that Hasan bin Ali himself settled about the end of the twelfth century.

Early settlements. The number of Muslims who settled on the coast must have been small, and such knowledge as we have of their life is based on archaeology, and the writings of Arab geographers. Excavations near Lamu are revealing that, by the tenth century, there was a wealthy settlement at Manda, with some impressive stone houses and a sea-wall built with the largest coral blocks found south of the Sahara. Iron smelting was carried on nearby, and a profusion of Islamic pottery suggests a busy trade with the Persian Gulf, but the absence of coins points to it being carried on by barter. Considerable excavations have also been made at Kilwa, which reveal a high standard of technical skill. Kilwa took the lead, and was the centre of a network of trade connections among the chief coastal settlements, which were at Kilwa, Tumbata, Pemba, Zanzibar, Vumba, the Lamu Archipelago and Mogadishu. Most of the towns probably began in the twelfth or thirteenth century. By the fifteenth century they were well laid out, with streets in which there were houses of stone and mortar, surrounded by land which was cultivated by slaves. In between the towns there were probably small settlements, with only a mosque and perhaps a headman's house built of stone and cemented with coral lime.

Kilwa. Map 3 shows that most of these places were on islands, although some of them, like Mombasa, were only separated from the mainland by a narrow stretch of water. This was because many of their settlers were people who were used to making their way as traders on the sea; even today, in Lamu men travel from place to place by dhow as they would by taxi in Mombasa. These islands were also all fortified and towns gradually grew up behind their defences. From the appearance of the ruins of these we think that many of their inhabitants were influenced by memories of homes in Arabia and Persia. To Kilwa, for instance, the knowledge of how to build in stone, carve wood and weave cottons seems to have been brought from Persia. By the end of the thirteenth century Kilwa entered a new era of prosperity, probably based on the very profitable gold-trade with Sofala, which she had long shared with Mogadishu. It seems likely that it was about then that she got a practical monopoly of this trade, and could afford to build the palace and trading-depot known as Husuni Kubwa as well as extend the great mosque. The former covered 2 acres, and included an ornamental swimming pool as well as avenues, terraces, and courtyards. The towns were always quarrelling among themselves, now one and now another taking the lead. Kilwa, however, always had an important position from the time when it was bought by Hasan bin Ali from the Africans. Guessing that the Africans meant to come back later and recapture it, Hasan is said to have dug a channel between the town and the mainland, thus making Kilwa an island, not only at high tide, but at all times. When he had also added fortifications, Kilwa became a strong place from which Hasan went on to control the coast from Sofala to Pemba. Its leading position at this time is illustrated by the fact that, in the reign of Hasan's son Ali, it was possible for Ali to appoint his son Muhammad to be governor of Mombasa. But by the time Vasco da Gama's ship reached Mombasa Kilwa had begun to decline, a process that was accelerated in 1505, when Portugal cut her off from the gold-trade with Sofala.

Trade in the Indian Ocean. By the fifteenth century Europe's demand for luxury goods was increasing; pepper and spices in particular were sought, and Arabia was the centre of the valuable maritime trade between the Far East, Mesopotamia and Persia, and the countries bordering the Mediterranean Sea. Chinese silks, Indian cotton cloth, rhubarb from China (valued for its medicinal properties), precious stones, pepper, nutmeg, mace, ginger and cloves were brought to Arabia by sea and sent thence by caravan across the desert, or transhipped up the Red Sea by the Arabs, who monopolised its navigation.

As well as being an important market-place for the traffic between East and West, Arabia annually sent a fleet of ships down the east coast of Africa, to carry on the trade in ivory, slaves, spices, tortoise-shell, skins, including leopard-skins for saddles, iron and millet, which had attracted the Arabs in the first place. While Africa was the chief source of the first two items, the only spices that were then obtained from East Africa were frankincense and cinnamon. Other spices, such as cloves, which came from the Malacca islands, and pepper, from India, were obtained in the Far East, where the merchants of East Africa and Arabia paid the local rulers for the right to have factories and agents. There was also a fair amount of East African trade in ambergris and gold. This last had its centre at Sofala, the nearest port to Zimbabwe. The Indians, who owned a good deal of the ocean shipping, also shared in this trade, and by the end of the Middle Ages trade relations between India and East Africa may have been as important as those between the East African coast and the Persian Gulf. Indians were probably the experts who dealt with finance and with the retail trade, for this is work for which they, unlike the Arabs, have long shown ability. Neither Indian nor Arab showed any desire to explore the vast continent which lay behind the coast. They were content to exchange the goods they brought, that is, their beads, glass, metal-work and cloth, for the ivory, ambergris, slaves and gold obtained from the interior.

THE RISE OF THE SWAHILI CULTURE

On the coast, the Arabs intermarried with the Africans. The result was that the Swahili people shared the faith of Islam and the mercantile way of life of the Arabs. The latter were few in number, and by the third generation probably spoke the Swahili language. It is difficult to tell the size of the population. While some towns, such as Kilwa and Mombasa had thousands of inhabitants, who shared considerable prosperity, life in the villages between was simpler. Here the houses would be huts of wattle and mud, with grass or *makuti* roofs, and fishing or agriculture the occupations; millet or rice were the usual grain crops. Simple homes like these were also usual in the town, but the wealthier merchants (and this was above all an Islamic and mercantile society) lived in considerable style; lemons, oranges, pomegranates and vegetables were grown in gardens watered from wells, and their homes were built of stone with flat roofs, entered through a sunken courtyard. The remains of the fine plaster decoration on some of these homes can still be seen.

The areas of the town in which the wealthy merchants lived probably resembled present-day Lamu, where the seashore is a hive of activity, and narrow lanes between blocks of buildings cut off heat from the sun. A report from Ibn Battuta, who visited the coast in the fourteenth century, suggests that the Swahili people ate well. The usual meal seemed to be a large dish of flesh, fish and fowl, laid over rice with milk and fruit. This would be served on imported, glazed Islamic ware, or possibly Chinese porcelain. Even the poorer people, by the fifteenth century, would have had their food in an eating-bowl, but it would not have been the lavish menu described above. As Ibn Battuta remarked, 'One of these people eats as much as several of us. It is their custom.'

The archaeological research which has been undertaken in the last few years on the east African coast has unearthed not only buildings and inscriptions, but also ceramics and coins. From evidence at Kilwa we know that cowrie shells, the early medium of exchange, had been replaced by coins by about 1200 A.D. when Ali bin al-Hasan, founder of the Shirazi dynasty, was sultan. His reign is usually taken as the prelude to the three centuries in which the Islamic civilisation on the coast reached its high-water mark. It was a civilisation based on sea-going trade, and extended inland only a short distance, possibly only 5 miles. Most of the towns had rulers who used a variety of titles, which were hereditary within the family, although it was not by any means always the eldest who became the next ruler. Some towns had a republican form of government, and in others either hereditary office-holders or influential councils restrained the rulers, who knew that they could be expelled.

This life on the coast was dependent on slaves who had been captured in the interior. Those who survived this journey to serve Arab masters in their plantations and homes were relatively fortunate, for the Koran taught Muslims that kindliness to slaves was a virtue, and many were as well treated as slaves can be. The more unfortunate were those who had still to face the horrors of a sea-passage in which they were packed so close together that they could hardly turn round. These included those who were shipped to Oman, to India and probably to China.

Early Mombasa. One interesting puzzle remains: what change occurred in the fortunes of Mombasa to account for its transformation from a town which Ibn Battuta described in 1331 as lacking in agriculture, having mosques built of wood and a bare-foot population, to the thriving city which Duarte Barbosa saw at the beginning of the sixteenth century? He wrote:

> There is a city of the Moors, called Bombaza [Mombasa] very large and beautiful, and built of high and handsome houses of stone and whitewash, and with very good streets, in the manner of those of Quiboa. And it also has a king over it. The people are of dusky white and brown complexions, and likewise the women, who are much adorned with silk and gold stuffs. It is a town of great trade in goods, and has a good port, where there are always many ships, both of those that sail for Sofala and those that come from Cambray and Melinde, and others which sail to the islands of Zanzibar, Manfia and Pemba. .. This Mombasa is a country well supplied with plenty of provisions, very fine sheep, which have round tails, and many cows, chickens and very large goats, much rice and millet, and plenty of oranges, sweet and bitter, and lemons, cedrates, pomegranates, Indian figs, and all sorts of vegetables, and very good water. The inhabitants at times are at war with the people of the continent (Mombasa itself is an island) and at other times at peace, and trade with them and obtain much honey and wax, and ivory.

This is not the only evidence we have for its prosperity. In 1506 Mombasa could offer the Portuguese viceroy of India, d'Almeida, a bribe of 50,000 *parados* of gold. This discrepancy in the descriptions was pointed out by the British historian, Roland Oliver, who suggests two possible explanations: in the interim Mombasa may have become the headquarters of Gujerat traders; or the trade brought by the ships from Cambray, which are referred to in the extract above, may hold the secret. The fact that no mediaeval coins have been found at Mombasa may point to a primitive economy, but it does not prove it, and the Swahili inhabitants may have found a means of sharing in the trade between the Middle East, India and the East African coast, for which it had a singularly good harbour, and the advantage of up-country connections.

The struggle for control. Such was the life lived in East Africa when the Portuguese Vasco da Gama rounded the Cape of Good Hope on his search for a new route to the spice islands of the East. The old overland routes from Europe to India had become more difficult to use since the Turks captured Constantinople in 1453. His arrival began three hundred years in which the main concern of the Swahili peoples was to preserve their independence from the threats to it from immigrant tribes and clans seeking shelter on the coastal fringe, and from the growing menace first of Portugal and later of Oman. During the first century Portugal was concerned with the east coast of Africa mainly as a supply-base for new ships on their way to the East, and was content to leave the towns under the control of their traditional Shirazi rulers. During this period, the chief threat came from the immigrant peoples who had begun to occupy the coastal area, particularly in the north where attacks from both land and sea overwhelmed some small settlements, which disappeared in these hard years. But from 1592 the Portuguese tightened their grip on the coast. Their hold was eventually undermined by local Swahili, with the help of allies from Oman, and the period of Omani Arab control of the coast glided into the era in which the sultan of Zanzibar was the key figure. A convenient date for the start of the new era is 1832, when Seyyid Said, the ruler of Oman began to live permanently in Zanzibar. Economic and commercial factors now replace the details of political strife, for Seyyid Said saw himself as a merchant whose influence travelled along the caravan routes. With the development of trade with the interior, East Africa entered the modern world. Further details of this development are given in Chapters 4 and 5, but first the chief features of the struggle for control of the coast must be outlined.

Arrival of Vasco da Gama. The Swahili states, among which Kilwa, Mombasa, Malindi and Pate were prominent, were accustomed to quarrel among themselves and unaccustomed to facing a foe from outside, particularly one equipped with greater resources, including guns, who worked to a master-plan. In 1498 da Gama saw the prosperous town of Malindi and was greeted by a king, 'wearing a robe of damask trimmed with green satin, and seated on two cushioned chairs of bronze'. He proved helpful, and supplied Vasco da Gama with a good pilot to guide him across the Indian Ocean to Calicut. This reception was the beginning of a long friendship between the Portuguese and Malindi, and was partly due to the bad feeling that existed between Mombasa and Malindi. Once it was known at Malindi that Vasco da Gama had been received badly in Mombasa, the king was eager to welcome him.

D'Albuquerque's plan for the Portuguese conquest. In 1499 Vasco da Gama returned to Portugal and told of his great discoveries. Portugal was quick to see the importance of these, and ten years later she had conquered the east coast of Africa and was able to appoint Dom Duarte de Lemos as governor of all the Portuguese possessions in Africa and Arabia. This conquest of the East African coast was part of the great plan of the ambitious Portuguese, d'Albuquerque, who had worked out his ideas before he became viceroy of India in 1509. At that time the Portuguese merchants were dependent for their share of the valuable spice-trade on the good-will of the local rulers in India, who allowed them to maintain warehouses and agents on their soil. D'Albuquerque realised that this precarious foothold could be converted into a maritime and Christian empire only if Portugal had a permanent fleet in the Indian Ocean. This meant that Portugal must have fortresses which would command the chief routes of the Indian Ocean trade. Once these had been conquered, she would cease to be dependent on a commerce that was trading without a licence, and had a far-distant base in Lisbon, and would rule a secure commercial empire covering the whole of the Middle East. Its centre was to be at Goa in India where the chief representative of Portugal, called the viceroy of India, would have his headquarters, and control the trade of the west coast of India. To guard the routes to India, d'Albuquerque reckoned that he must gain control of three places: Socotra, which was to be a base for ventures into the Red Sea, and so useful for the interception of spice cargoes (he would have preferred Aden, but it proved impossible to capture); Ormuz, which controlled the entry to the Persian Gulf and was one of the most important markets in the world for eastern products; and Malacca, which was the western end of the Chinese trade, and the only place from which the Portuguese could control all the trade, mostly in spices, across the Bay of Bengal. But it was not enough for Portugal to conquer these places; she had to think also of supplying her sailing-ships on their long voyages to the East. For this it was essential for her to conquer the East

African coast, and between 1500 and 1509 this was done, with great savagery.

Beginning of the Portuguese conquest. The first step was taken by Vasco da Gama on his second voyage to India, in 1502. He called at Kilwa and forced the sultan to pay a yearly tribute to the king of Portugal. This was typical of Portugal's dealings with the coast. Tribute was demanded and unless it was paid the town was destroyed. If it was paid the local sultan was usually left in peace, provided he carried out the wishes of the Portuguese. After Kilwa, Zanzibar was the next place to suffer from the Portuguese. In 1503 a Portuguese commander called Ravasco showed the power of guns by using two boats with cannon to defeat canoes carrying 4,000 men. These canoes had been manned by the ruler of Zanzibar, in protest against Ravasco's unprovoked attack on a number of small local ships carrying goods that Ravasco wanted.

D'Almeida. This was only the beginning. In 1505 a fleet of more than twenty ships set sail from Portugal for India. The newly-appointed viceroy of India, d'Almeida, was in command, and his first task was to gain control of three key places on the coast of East Africa: Sofala, Kilwa and Mombasa. Sofala was important to the Portuguese because it would give them control of the gold supply. It offered hardly any resistance, and a fort was built to protect the Portuguese colony that now replaced the old Arab settlement. But the Portuguese inability to co-operate with either Arab or African was their undoing here, and in a few years Sofala could barely pay its way. Nor was its old overlord, Kilwa, in better shape; cut off from the gold-trade with Sofala, which had supplied much of its prosperity, it sank into a decline which only ended when the Zimba swarmed into the town and killed the inhabitants. A Dominican friar on the coast at the end of the sixteenth century wrote of the Zimba that they 'worship no God, nor Idol, but their King, who (they say) is God of the Earth; and if it rains when he would not, they shoot their arrows at the sky for not obeying him . . . They eate those which they kill in warre.'

Having laid waste Kilwa, d'Almeida's fleet then sailed away to deal with Mombasa, which of late had secured a larger share of trade than Kilwa; so that by 1505 Kilwa had only 4,000 inhabitants, compared to Mombasa's 10,000. Unlike Sofala and Kilwa, Mombasa did not yield without a fight, and throughout the 200 years during which the Portuguese ruled in East Africa, she was to be a thorn in their side, an island well-named the 'Island of war'. But the bowmen of Mombasa could not long resist guns and armour, and Mombasa too was conquered, and set on fire. Its resilience, though, was remarkable and may have been due not only to its favourable trading situation but also to its position as a mainland power as well as an island state. This position gave it the support of inland tribes in times of crisis.

Not one of these three places, Sofala, Kilwa and Mombasa, however, was to be the headquarters of the Portuguese on the east coast. They found it more convenient to rule from Mozambique, which was 'colonised' in 1507. The Portuguese representative on the north of the East African coast was the captain of Malindi.

Bases of the Portuguese empire. When d'Albuquerque died in 1515, six years after the first Portuguese governor-general of the coast had been appointed, he left his country ruling an empire in the Indian Ocean which had its supply bases on the east coast of Africa, the chief of which was Mozambique. The headquarters of this empire was at Goa, the most important of the Portuguese trading stations on the west coast of India. It included Malacca, parts of Ceylon, a number of places in the Malay Archipelago, Socotra, Muscat in Oman and Ormuz, which guards the entry to the Persian Gulf. Aden alone had successfully resisted the Portuguese. The importance of Portuguese conquests lay in their value as trading centres or as forts guarding their empire.

Results of the Portuguese conquest. From the beginning the Portuguese found the East African part of their empire disappointing, because it never brought them the wealth they had expected. They had hoped to secure this by cutting off Arab trade with India, and by attacking the Arab coastal trade, both on sea and land. They intended to deal direct with the Africans themselves, and no share of their profits was to be taken by Arab or Indian middlemen. So the Portuguese were content to fill their warehouses with calico and beads from India and wait for the Africans to bring gold, ivory and slaves from the interior. The Portuguese under-estimated the importance of the local traders and they also lacked the men to staff these caravans. It must also be remembered that they were not interested in setting up administrative machinery in their bases, and they never had enough Portuguese to staff them. Consequently the supply of ivory and slaves dried up and the Sofala gold-trade, which supported the prosperity of the East Coast, was diverted south with disastrous results. The old Arab settlements, which had been taken over by the Portuguese became poorer and weaker. This was most marked in the south, where Mozambique, Kilwa and Sofala had their Portuguese garrisons and forts. Things were a little easier in the north, where local sultans were still allowed to rule, provided they paid the annual tribute, but even here the conquerors were hated, and the Africans called the chief of the Portuguese '*afriti*', or devil.

Unrest in Mombasa. Mombasa was the leader in most of the trouble that arose from this hatred, and as she was unpopular with some of her neighbours, for example, Malindi and Zanzibar, they sometimes helped the Portuguese to punish her. In 1528, for instance, both Malindi and Zanzibar helped Nuno da Cunha to attack Mombasa while he was on his way to India to take up his post as viceroy. The result was that Mombasa had to pay a large sum of gold as tribute every year, and when the town tried to avoid this it was burnt to the ground. After this the 'Island of War' gave no trouble until 1586, when a Turkish pirate called Mirale Bey came sailing down the coast looking for loot. He told the people of Mombasa that he had been sent by the sultan to rescue them, and he did in fact drive the Portuguese out of most of their settlements. He then sailed away, and it was not long before the viceroy at Goa heard from Malindi what had happened. Punishment followed swiftly, but the spirit of Mombasa was not crushed. Three years later the people again welcomed Mirale Bey on his return to the coast. The viceroy of India also heard the news, and sent a fleet of ships to prevent another rebellion. Although Mirale Bey had come fairly well-equipped this time, with five ships, he knew that it would be very difficult to hold Mombasa against the Portuguese, and therefore accepted help offered by the Zimba. This was a Bantu tribe who had been moving up Africa since they left their lands near Zululand. They had captured Kilwa (see page 28) and were certain that if they waited for their chance they would be able to cross to the island of Mombasa, and enjoy the feast that the fine town offered. Mirale Bey mistrusted them, but he could not resist accepting their offer of help against the Portuguese, and allowed them to cross to the island. No sooner were they there than they turned on the inhabitants, many of whom flung themselves desperately into the sea, where sharks were waiting for them.

Fort Jesus. Although the Portuguese put down this rebellion by Mombasa, the island continued to give trouble, and so in 1592 they again attacked, and largely destroyed the town. This time they deposed the sultan and put the sultan of Malindi in his place, because they hoped that, as Malindi had always been loyal to them, Mombasa under his rule would cease to give trouble. This they considered important, for there was no doubt that the town was in a very strong position; and with the change of rulers they decided to make it the capital of their East African lands. To guard their new capital Fort Jesus was built, looking out over the harbour.

The decline of Portuguese power. By the end of the sixteenth century the first English ships had begun to appear in the Indian Ocean. They were the forerunners of the British East India Company, and were disliked by the Portuguese, who dreaded any interference with their trade monopoly in this area, especially as they knew that their hold on the coast was weakening. There were several reasons for this. In the first place Portugal never had a large enough population to carry out all her colonial plans. Two million people were not sufficient to cultivate Portugal, as well as control Brazil and the empire in the Indian Ocean. Such energy as they had was devoted to Brazil rather than East Africa, which was not a place where many Portuguese settled, even temporarily. In addition, many of the Portuguese settlers in East Africa died from tropical diseases. Others were killed in the continual fighting on the coast. In 1580 Philip II, king of Spain, inherited the throne of Portugal, and as he had already more lands to administer than he was capable of dealing with, the affairs of Portugal took second place. Thus, by the end of the sixteenth century, Portugal's grasp on the coast of Africa was feeble. She had long been hated in her empire, where the conquered people could not forgive her greed and cruelty. They were quick, therefore, to seize every chance of rebellion.

The establishment of Omani power. The first serious revolt to succeed was in Ormuz, where, in 1622, the Persians drove out the Portuguese. When this news spread down the East African coast it encouraged a feeling of restlessness, and in 1631 Mombasa, as usual, was the first to rebel. The leader was the Sultan Yusuf, who had been brought up as a Catholic by the Portuguese and educated at Goa. In India he grew familiar with the Portuguese way of life, and ended by despising it. Soon after his appointment as sultan of Mombasa Yusuf became a Muslim. In a few months he was complaining, with justice, of the way in which the Portuguese governor of Mombasa ruled. By 1631 he was plotting against the Portuguese, and then managed to lead 300 of his followers into Fort Jesus, where he stabbed the governor. Although Yusuf followed this up by behaviour as savage as that of the Portuguese at their worst, his lead was followed by Pemba and other places on the coast. When it looked as if the forces from Goa would be successful in reconquering Mombasa, Yusuf himself dismantled the fort and destroyed it before sailing away to Arabia. Thus Mombasa lost its last sultan. The years of the Portuguese empire in the east were numbered.

The British and the Dutch East India Companies were replacing the Portuguese traders on the eastern shores of the Indian Ocean, and one by one Portugal's strong places were taken from her. Oman too had followed Ormuz in driving out her Portuguese conquerors, who now had only East Africa left of their empire in the East. Even that was not to be theirs long; for Mombasa was quick to appeal to the Sultan bin Seif, who as imam of Oman was the religious head of his country as well as its ruler, to come to the rescue of his fellow-Muslims. Sultan bin Seif answered this appeal by freeing Mombasa from the Portuguese. However, owing to revolts in Oman he had to leave the town to be recaptured, and it was his son, the Iman Seif bin Sultan, who finally captured Fort Jesus, and became master of Mombasa in 1698. In 1699 he drove the Portuguese out of Kilwa, and Pemba also, and this date is usually counted as marking the end of Portuguese rule in East Africa, north of Mozambique where they still rule.

The results of Portuguese rule. Considering they were in a dominant position on the East African coast for 200 years, the Portuguese did very little for the country beyond building Fort Jesus, but it must be remembered that they were not interested in setting up administrative machinery in their bases and they never had enough Portuguese stationed in the area to pass on their culture; their main contribution, and it was a valuable one, consisted in introducing manioc, pineapples, paw-paws, guavas, ground-nuts, and sweet potatoes which enriched the diet of many East Africans. Their limited contribution may also have been due to the fact that there were never more than a hundred Portuguese living north of Cape Delgado, and the hatred these inspired checked any impulse to imitate them. In addition it may have been because they were never really interested in the land, except as a useful stopping-place on the way to India. In fact the chief result of their rule was that it crippled the old Arab settlements, which lost their wide trade interests, and became decaying towns off the main shipping-routes, whose only political link with the outside world was that with the imam of Muscat, who ruled Zanzibar.

The Mazrui. Like his father, Seif bin Sultan was called back by one of the revolts which always seemed to break out when a ruler left Oman. He had, therefore, to leave various Omani Arabs to rule the coastal settlements in East Africa. In Mombasa, for instance, he left the head of the Mazrui family, and in 1741 a change of dynasty in Oman gave the Mazrui governor in charge an opportunity to establish an independent sheikdom, which was to last almost a hundred years and give Mombasa a dominating position on the coast. While her only rival, Pate, was torn by civil wars, the Mazrui held the balance between rival factions in Mombasa and provided the security which enabled her to develop a foreign policy and acquire a set of Nyika alliances, besides acting as a refuge for townsmen from the rest of the coast. Towards the end of the eighteenth century Pate and Mombasa achieved a working partnership, in which the latter led. The threat to their practical independence came from Oman, whose imam had not yielded his sovereignty over the coast. As long as he interpreted this to mean little more than assistance against his foreign enemies the coastal states did not dispute it. The powerful Mazrui family also controlled Pemba, which was their principal source of food. Trouble began in 1807 with a disputed succession in Pate in which many of the supporters of the unsuccessful candidate fled to Lamu. After an unsuccessful attack by the Mazrui on Lamu, the inhabitants appealed for help to Seyyid Said, imam of Oman, whose control of the coast had been slipping away, except in Zanzibar, Mafia and, later, in Kilwa. Lamu's appeal and implied submission gave the imam a base off the coast further north than Zanzibar and weakened Pate's position, where one of their perennial dynastic quarrels enabled Seyyid Said, in 1822, to end the Mazrui influence there. The stage was now set for the real struggle; later in the year Pemba was captured from the Mazrui, but the key to the coast remained Mombasa with its good harbour protected by Fort Jesus. The Mazrui, however, made a last desperate bid to remain independent of Oman by offering the protectorate of Mombasa to Britain. The story of this offer and its final rejection, is told in Chapter 5. Finally a split among the Mazrui gave the ruler of Oman his chance. He got control of Fort Jesus in 1837, and in a few months he was the unquestioned ruler of Mombasa.

During the years in which Said had been concentrating on the capture of Mombasa he had grown very attached to the island of Zanzibar, which had loyally supported all his efforts, and in 1832 he made it his real capital.

Seyyid Said's reign: a watershed. On Seyyid Said's death the tie with Oman was finally cut, Oman going to his eldest son while the second son inherited Zanzibar. This symbolised a more fundamental change in the history of the coast, which was no longer to turn on policies or actions, shaped in Europe or the Middle East, that disregarded the interior which the growing caravan trade was penetrating. Zanzibar's merchant–sultan had triggered off an expansion of trade which was to strengthen the links between the coast and the interior and finally sever the tie with Oman and the Middle East. But when the Suez Canal was cut in 1869, and the coast brought over 4,000 miles nearer to the gate of Europe, it looked as if Oman's influence was going to be replaced by that of Britain and Germany, who were beginning to take an interest in the development of East Africa. During the reign of Seyyid Barghash, 1870–88, there was a development in communications, which in East Africa has usually been the prelude to increased material prosperity. A monthly mail-service, between Zanzibar and Aden, was introduced by the British Steam Navigation Company (now the British India Company) which provided a link with the rapidly improving steamship service between England and India. Then in 1897 the Eastern Telegraph Company speeded up communications further by laying a submarine cable from Aden to Zanzibar. Britain's thoughts, however, were elsewhere: with the balance of power in Europe; with Egypt and the control of the Nile; with the glittering splendour of her Indian empire and the problems presented by South Africa; while German expansion was to be frustrated by two World Wars. In East Africa, Britain's main concern was to stop slavery; other problems were looked at in the light of diplomatic considerations, or administrative convenience.

Chapter 3

THE FORMATION OF
EAST AFRICAN STATES

'Change', it has been said, 'is the essence of history', and it is important to realise that in the centuries before the coming of Europeans, East African society was changing and evolving under the pressure of trade, war, migration and the interaction of pastoralists and agriculturalists. In Chapters 1 and 2 we have described the growth of the coastal states and the early settlements in the interior. In this chapter the evolution of states in the interior of East Africa is described, as an example of the kind of development that was taking place before the coming of Europeans on a large scale.

The Ngoni invasion. In southern Tanganyika until the middle of the nineteenth century, many of the inhabitants were shifting cultivators; others were hunters and fishermen. This was a region which had not apparently been influenced by either the Nilo-Hamitic or Nilotic peoples. It was here that the last large-scale immigration before the coming of the Europeans occurred. The invaders were the Ngoni, who moved away from Natal in South Africa to avoid being absorbed in Chaka's cruel empire. They crossed the Zambezi in 1835, and the main body settled for a time on the plateau just above the south-east corner of Lake Tanganyika. On their journey they had been, often against their will, joined by the survivors of other defeated peoples, and after the death of Zwangendaba, the Ngoni leader, in about 1848, they broke up into smaller raiding bodies. Some of these gathered up tribal groups, which they found small and disorganised, and incorporated them into new Ngoni states; and a number of their neighbours now sought strength through closer union; among these were the Hehe. Others suffered from the hordes of raiders and refugees who were let loose; these formed bands of mercenary warriors, called *ruga-ruga,* who joined any leader holding out hopes of rich plunder. They usually wore red cloaks, feather head-dresses and ornaments of copper and ivory. Beyond building their leader's house and stronghold, they were not prepared to do any work; they reckoned to live on what their guns won for them, and by the middle of the nineteenth century there was a steady flow of these weapons from Zanzibar into the interior. These guns fascinated a young Nyamwezi warrior, who was very successful in supplying his force of *ruga-ruga* with them. A man of great courage and clear aims, Mirambo, as the warrior was called, was also helped by speaking the language of the Ngoni, and may even have been brought up among them as a captive. His ancestors probably included a well-known leader of the Nyamwezi, but his father only owned Ugogwe; to this Mirambo added territory belonging to his mother's family. Mirambo had the advantage of knowing exactly what he wanted, which was to control all the commercial routes of the lake regions. He began his acquisitive career early in the sixties.

Trade and Mirambo. At this time, there were two main Arab settlements. The first was in the region around Tabora, where the Arab market of Unyanyembe was situated; here well-travelled lines led northwards to Lake Nyanza and the powerful kingdoms of Uganda and met those used by travellers bringing with them iron and slaves. Its central position and comparatively security made Unyanyembe the headquarters of the Arabs, many of whom settled there for years in charge of depots, while their slaves and factors travelled round collecting articles for trade; these included ivory, men and pretty women. The other main settlement was at Ujiji on the shore of Lake Tanganyika which a missionary described as 'quite a little Egypt'; representatives of all the tribes came to it for trade and diplomatic purposes. There was frequent communication between these two settlements, and the Arabs were also concerned to keep open the routes to the north, where the powerful kabaka of Buganda ruled. Caravan leaders knew that the friendship of most of the small chiefs along the trade-routes could be won by handfuls of beads, or a few yards of cloth, but Mirambo presented a more serious problem. He was determined that all the caravans should cross his country and so have to pay dues to him. As his land lay across the easiest route from Ujiji to Tabora, he soon began also to control a part of the road to Victoria Nyanza. This policy was a direct threat to Arab profits, and they sought allies against him. These included the explorer, Stanley, but Stanley was more concerned with meeting Livingstone. He stayed in the fight long enough, however, to give his impression of Mirambo, whom he called a Napoleon, impressed perhaps by the terrified respect with which he was regarded. He was so continuously victorious that his contemporaries thought of him as almost supernatural and, as Stanley wrote, 'Immediately the cry "Mirambo! Mirambo!" is raised from every height the alarming cry is echoed, until from Usih to Usanda and from Masai north to Usomao, the dread name is repeated.' He was not, however, invincible; he never extended his lands as widely as he wanted to in Usuhuma and was often content with a vague overlordship. Secure in this, he offered merchants a safe passage in return for payment, the cost of which is said

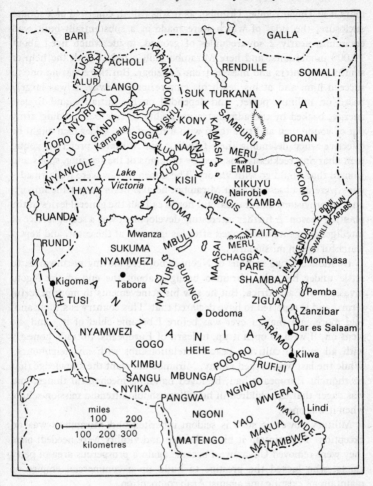

Map 4   The peoples of East Africa

to have doubled the price of ivory. Those who resisted were plundered without mercy and the pick of their young men taken as recruits for his army. Once his conquest was accepted Mirambo seems to have treated his victims reasonably well and to have aimed at attaching them to himself.

Mirambo's achievements. By 1884, when he died of laryngitis, he too had an impressive capital, strong enough to challenge the rival Arab market at Unyanyembe. Urambo, as it was called, consisted of a square enclosure, the sides of which were made of a substantially-built wall encircling nearly 2 square miles of ground, inside which lived about 15,000 inhabitants; and here Mirambo built a palace with the help of smiths, carpenters and masons from Zanzibar. But there was no one to succeed him, and at his death his empire melted away. It was largely based on military power, and depended on his initiative and tireless energy, backed by the administrative ability to create a standing army out of young men and rule them with a rod of iron. Older men might be effective when defending their families, but Mirambo preferred young men charging recklessly, inspired by thoughts of the feasting, spoils and women that would go with victory. These men he saw were well armed – guns were an obsession with Mirambo; he also never forgot the importance of provisions and was careful not to call out the general levies in the planting season. A further interesting development was a secret service of intelligence agents who looked after his interests at the coast, and kept a watchful eye on missionaries.

By inducing two sections of Ngoni, who were moving northwards, to settle under his rule, Mirambo brought about the end of the Ngoni invasions of East Africa. But he saw his achievements in more peaceful terms, and is reported to have declared that 'This country is a thousand-fold more safe than it ever was before I became chief of it.' And, he went on, 'I wish to open it up, to learn of Europeans, to trade honestly with all and to cultivate peaceful relationships with my neighbours.' While the last wish lacked reality, Mirambo did want the knowledge that he thought Europeans had; he loved handling mechanical things, and was eager that the children in his village should attend a mission school when it was open.

Military power as such is seldom inherited and Mirambo's was no exception. To maintain it his leadership and vitality were needed; once they were removed Unyamwezi became again a prosperous area of petty chiefs, who lacked the prestige to build up a commercial empire or maintain an existing one against Arab competition.

Rise of Ntemi chiefdoms. A Ntemi chief was one who could cut a discussion short and give his decision. From Skuma-Unyamwezi Ntemi chiefdoms spread to the east of Lake Victoria, and by the mid-eighteenth century were found in Gogoland and the area between Morogoro and Kilimanjaro; it is perhaps significant that at least three of the Chagga chiefdoms have an ancestor called Ntemi. According to old traditions a cattle-owning people, moving south-eastwards, had introduced the institution of chiefs, with other new ideas, and the uniformity of chiefs' customs in this area points to a common origin, probably in the interlacustrine region. The difference between the regions lies in the size of the area administered by the chiefs. In western Tanzania, it was restricted to an area that could be administered by the close relations of the ruler: but in the interlacustrine region it was very much larger. The institution of Ntemi chiefdoms spread from the north as far south as Tanzania. This institution gave the chief the ritual of a divine king, who must not be seen to die. He had to be buried with special ceremonies, for he held the royal fire from which all other fire was kindled. When Mbega, chief of the Kilindi who lived in Tanga province, died, a chronicler wrote, 'The day of his death was known only by five elders. He was sick for only three days, and his children did not hear of it, nor even the people there in the town.' The same chronicler describes his selection as chief:

> A man of Vulga said, The matter is ended, he is our King. Let us bring him out and take his hand and let all the people see him. They brought him out into the courtyard to the multitude and took his hand to signify that he was indeed their judge, and they proclaimed, Every word that he says we accept, if any man is disobedient, let him die, we will kill him by universal consent.

Kimweri. Kimweri, known to his subjects as Simba wa Muene or 'Lion of Heaven' was an outstanding sultan of Vuga. He was born about 1800, and by 1840 ruled a kingdom which included most of the Pare and Usambara Mountains, and reached to the coast itself. Moreover, if one of the coastal people was chosen as a chief he had to come to Kimweri to receive his turban before his accession was recognised. The southern boundary of his kingdom was the Pangani River, beyond which the firearms of the Zigu prevented further advance. All the same, Kimweri's kingdom had half a million people and comprised an area similar to a parallelogram 140 miles long and 60 miles wide.

He ruled it with an iron hand. Taxes, usually in cloth, had to be paid, even though hut-owners hastily buried their valuables when the soldiers collecting them appeared. Discipline was swift and strong. Disobedience meant instant selling into slavery. No one was allowed to rival the king in grandeur; it was illegal to ride on a horse or donkey, to wear expensive clothes, or to travel far from home. No one cared to look rich for fear of appearing to rival the king in wealth. Only on the coast, where the people might have turned the Arabs against him, was there some relaxation of the strictness of Kimweri's rule. There the Swahili were exempt from taxation, and could ride and wear expensive clothes if they wished. They even called themselves the Wangwana or 'Free People'.

A missionary called Krapf, who visited Kimweri in 1848 and 1852, was most impressed. He noticed the efficiency and discipline as soon as he crossed the frontier into Usambara, because his entry, his route, his timetable and his departure were all organised and fixed. Every movement was laid down. But there were assets as well as restrictions. He was given an official guide, soldiers were detailed to carry his baggage, and free food was provided at every village. True, he was expected to give the king a present; but this was a small price to pay for so many conveniences. Krapf could hardly praise Kimweri enough. 'Never before had a journey been made so easy for me', he wrote; and he went on to say, 'As regards security, I do not believe that one could be safer in any European country than in Usambara.'

In his court at Vuga, Kimweri had two main officials to help him. They were the *mdoe* (or vizier) and the *mboki* (or military chief). In addition he divided his kingdoms into districts and put a governor, usually one of his sons, in charge of each. Every governor had to send a representative, called a *mlau,* to Kimweri's court, and it was through the *mlau* that the governor would transact his business. Sometimes Kimweri delegated his authority to his daughters also, for Krapf speaks of them as ruling various villages.

Along the coast we have already seen that Kimweri had to handle his kingdom with more discretion, because in this region his authority overlapped with that of the sultan of Zanzibar, whose commercial activity made its busy way into Usambara, as elsewhere. Tanga remained under the exclusive control of the sultan through a governor, but along the rest of the northern coastal strip Kimweri asserted his authority by appointing headmen known as *diwanis*. Their appointment was confirmed by the sultan. This solution seemed to please everyone. The sultan's trade continued, Kimweri's authority was acknowledged, and the *diwanis* themselves had the special privileges of being entitled to carry an umbrella of state and walk about accompanied by a band of music.

Kimweri died about 1860. A period of internal strife followed and his kingdom diminished, but its fame was so proudly remembered that when Sir Donald Cameron, who was then the British governor of Tanganyika (see page 156) was reviving tribal authorities in the 1920s, Africans from the mountains to the coast were anxious to be considered descendants of Kimweri's subjects.

Uganda. Between the seventeenth and the nineteenth centuries the history of Uganda is dominated by that of the loosely-knit kingdom of Bunyoro, and its satellite states. The establishment of a Bito dynasty, as

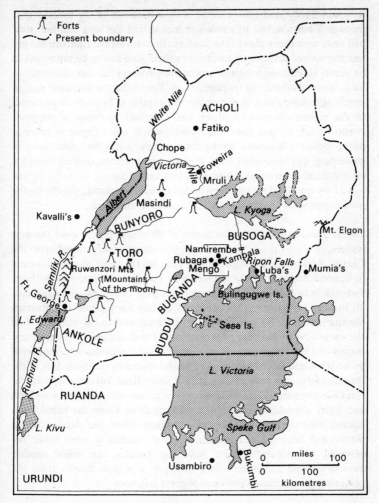

Map 5 The peoples of Uganda

a result of Luo migration, in Bunyoro, was described in Chapter 1. Adventurous members of this ruling group were addicted to cattle-raids, which led to the establishment of Bito dynasties giving only ritual acknowledgement to the overlordships of Bunyoro; among these sub-dynasties was Buganda. The first of the Bito rulers of Buganda was Kimwera, who appears to have left Bunyoro under pressure from the Luo invaders in about the sixteenth century; his new kingdom was minute –

it would have fitted into a circle with a diameter of 50 miles drawn through Kampala, but its small size meant that the king and his circle had links with every clan in the country. By contrast the Banyoro did not feel themselves sufficiently involved in their kingdom to be interested in its survival. Although by the seventeenth century further immigration had nearly doubled the population of Buganda, the increase was in people sufficiently akin to the earlier inhabitants to be easily assimilated. In the eighteenth century, there was a further extension of territory north-westwards, this time into Busoga, which was completely overrun in the region of Kyaboga. In the next century, it was Buganda's turn to go raiding; by this time its rival, Bunyoro, had been weakened: firstly by an unfortunate campaign into Karagwe and Ndorwa; secondly by the loss of its iron-bearing territory to Ankole and Buganda; thirdly by the preoccupation of her kings with cattle rather than ruling.

The political and social organisation of Buganda. By the time the new powers, of whom the Arabs were the forerunners, had entered upon the Central African scene Buganda had built up the most advanced society in Central Africa and was the strongest power north and west of Lake Victoria. It had the great advantage of a steady annual rainfall of at least 30 inches. This enabled the Baganda to rely for food on the plantain banana and leave its cultivation for the most part to the women, while the men saw to building, the making of well-designed weapons and canoes and the developing of an elaborate state organisation, supported by taxation and forced labour. The feudal system of the early days of the Bito dynasty was now changing into centralised bureaucracy. At the head was the kabaka, who was elected by an assembly of the great chiefs and court officials. Usually the candidates from whom the kabaka was elected were the sons of the previous kings. When the election to the throne had been decided the unsuccessful candidates were either imprisoned or executed. Apart from the kabaka, the queen mother (*namasole*) and the queen-sister (*lubaga*), who was chosen from the princesses, also occupied positions of great influence.

Chiefs. One of the bureaucratic innovations was a council (*lukiko*) composed of great chiefs (*bakungu*) who were non-hereditary officials appointed by the king. The most important of these great chiefs were those who ruled the four main districts other than Buganda proper. In addition to these, and other, less important, great chiefs, there were also officials in the royal household, who were considered to rank as chiefs. Among these were the chief butler (*musenero*) and the chief baker (*mufumbiro*). All great chiefs had to spend several months each year at the king's capital, Kibuga, where each would have some honorary office. The rest of their time would be spent in their own province, where they acted as petty kings, each having his own body of officials, including a second-in-command, a head of slaves, a head of the upholsterers, and a chief of the gate-keepers. In addition each had a large number of wives, pages and slaves. From their subjects the chiefs were entitled to collect taxes, and in time of war it was the chief's duty to lead the army. When a chief died he would be wound in strips of bark-cloth and buried in one of his houses.

The sub-chiefs ('bataka'). Besides the great chiefs there were also the heads of clans (*bataka*). As clan elders they were guardians of clan lands, and formed an important class in Buganda, their position being an hereditary one and not depending on royal appointment like that of the great chiefs; but by the end of the century their power had been curbed, partly by means of agents appointed by the kabaka, who reported back to him.

The peasants ('bakopi'). Far below them came the great peasant class (*bakopi*). They attached themselves to chiefs, and in theory were allowed to change their service from one master to another if they wished; in fact such a change would usually be followed by severe punishment from the deserted chief. The main duty of the peasant was to follow his chief to war, which was for him an affair of tremendous suffering: small-pox took a very large toll of soldiers, and almost as many lives were lost in obtaining slaves as there were slaves obtained. At home the peasants' work consisted of cultivation and building houses. In return for his services the peasant would be given one, or possibly two wives, by the chief, but these were loaned rather than given permanently, and might be taken away by the chief at any time.

The slaves ('badu'). The lowest class were the slaves (*badu*). These were mostly drawn from the raids on the neighbouring countries of Bunyoro to the north-west and Busoga to the east. Each would be worth an average of 15,000 cowrie shells (about £5). They had no rights, and Mackay, the greatest of all the early Buganda missionaries, mentions an instance when a chief with whom he was dining killed his slave for upsetting a gourd of cider. In general the slaves were used for cultivation and for service in the houses of the king and the chiefs.

Occupations, clothing, and housing. The Baganda were essentially a fighting people, but nevertheless a considerable standard had been reached in peaceful occupations. One of their chief staples of wealth was bark-cloth made from the bark of a type of fig tree; and bead-work, which was exclusively a woman's occupation, had reached a remarkable standard. The houses in which the Baganda lived were beehive-shaped structures of grass, supported by wooden poles. The importance of the person to whom the house belonged could be estimated from its size.

Religion. The religion of Buganda was chiefly a mixture of witchcraft and ancestor-worship known as Lubaalism. Underlying this was the vague idea of a sublime creator, Katonda, of whom nothing was known and from whom nothing was expected. Next came Lubaale, the upper air and waters, including the gods who inhabited them. The chief of these gods who inhabited the upper air and waters was Mukasa, the god of Lake Victoria, who was responsible for the lives of sailors, all of whom tried to win his favour by throwing offerings of bananas into the lake, before starting a voyage. Lubaale was also the giver of wealth and the giver of children. Among the many demi-gods, Kintu, the traditional hero–king, was outstanding.

Contact with the outside world. During Kyaboga's reign, which ended about 1780, the first contact with the outside world was made, when cups and plates were brought in by way of Karagwe. Before the end of the century further articles, including cotton cloth, copper wire, and cowrie shells, also arrived by the same route. The arrival of the first Arabs in 1848–52 is described in Chapter 5. In 1862 the first European, Speke, arrived, and left us his impression of the court of the kabaka.

> Today the king sent his pages to announce his intention of holding a levee in my honour. I prepared for my first presentation at court, attired in my best, though in it I cut a poor figure in comparison with the display of the dressy Waganda. They wore neat bark-cloaks resembling the best yellow corduroy cloth, crimped and well-set as if stiffened with starch, and over that as upper-cloaks, a patch-work of small antelope skins, which I observed were sewn together as well as any English glovers could have pieced them; while their head-dresses, generally, were abrus turbans, set off with highly polished boar tusks, stick-charms, seeds, beads or shells; and on their necks, arms and ankles they wore other charms of wood.

Because early explorers were surprised to find a society as advanced as this in Africa they sometimes tended to represent Buganda as better than it really was. But there was little resemblance to Paradise in the kingdom over which the Kabakas Mutesa and Mwanga ruled. Each was a despot with no regard for human life. When Speke first showed Mutesa his gun the king immediately ordered a page to go outside and test its efficiency by shooting at the first man he saw, and he was delighted to hear that the man had been killed. On a picnic to the lake one of Mutesa's wives playfully offered him a fruit, and he immediately ordered that she should be executed because, he said, it was the first time a woman had ever had the impudence to offer him anything.

Fig. 3 A banyan looking at his account book – a sketch from Speke's
The Discovery of the Source of the Nile

Political systems of the Nilo-Hamitic peoples. In the nineteenth century, although the Maasai dominated a long wedge of land (see Map 4), their interests were limited to cattle and warfare; the possession of land, apart from the control of grazing- and water-rights, did not interest them. Cattle-raiding could be justified by an old legend which told how the Maasai earned the right to all the cattle on earth so that, 'If cattle are seen in the possession of Bantu tribes it is presumed that they have been stolen or found, and the Maasai say: "These are our animals, let us go and take them, for God in olden days gave us all the cattle upon the earth."' Warfare was their other main interest, and the education of their young men centred on their prowess as warriors; to prove himself a man, each had to kill a lion. In the nineteenth century the tribe was torn by complex civil wars between the different sub-clans, who grouped themselves round different *laibons*. These *laibons* had many of the attributes of witch-doctors and exercised a good deal of power through their influence over the strategy of war. Akin to the Maasai were their neighbours, the Nandi, who shared their warlike ambitions and developed a similar form of leadership to the Maasai *laibons* in their *orkoiyots*. These seem to have given the Nandi a courage in battle which enabled them to become the most dangerous people between the Rift Valley and Lake Victoria.

The Eastern Bantu. Secure in their forested highlands, the Kikuyu found that cutting down the trees gave them a fertile soil that grew more food than many of their neighbours enjoyed. Their numbers grew, and today the Kikuyu are the largest tribe in Kenya. Kikuyu legends tell of a time when the women ruled, until the men revolted and introduced a system of chieftainship. This was eventually replaced by an age-group system in which a council of elders held office till the younger generation of warriors had reached the wisdom of maturity. The hilly nature of most of the Kikuyu country made it natural for government to be centred on the ridges, but a link between the peoples of the ridges was often supplied by prominent individuals. Such a one was chief Wangombe, who came to power not by right of birth, for prominent positions among the Kikuyu were not inherited, but by his prowess as a hunter and a leader of warriors against the Maasai. Having become an elder, he encouraged harmony between the peoples of the different ridges by sending groups of trusted men round the whole country.

There is no record of chiefs among the Kamba: the tribe was broken up into a number of small groups, in even the largest of which the members lived within easy walking-distance of each other. They were presided over by the *nzama ya ndua* (council of elders) which was made up of the chief elders of the group, each of whom had to pay for admission to it. The chief function of this council was to act as a court of law, but it was also responsible for religious observances. That is why these councils usually centred round places of sacrifice. Nowadays a council like this might be expected to pass new laws, but the Kamba did not think this was necessary. This was partly because laws only come in with change. If there are no big changes, men will expect their neighbours to be guided by the established customs of the tribe or group. This is particularly true if a man is interested only in a small area. Again, in the early days of many countries laws were really better described as the orders of one person.

CHAPTER 4

AFRICA AND A WIDER WORLD

Geographical obstacles. Until modern times, deserts have been as serious an obstacle in the way of men's movements as the oceans over which they learnt to sail, the mountains they climbed and the forests through which they pushed their way for hundreds of years. That is why the Sahara divided Africa into two: a northern, Muslim portion linked with Mediterranean Europe, consisting of Egypt, Libya, Tripoli, Tunis and Morocco; and the grasslands and forests of tropical Africa, which in their turn are linked with the sub-tropical countries of South Africa and Rhodesia.

The inaccessible interior. The second of these areas was further isolated because travel from the sea was hindered by the scarp edges of the plateau which forms the interior of Africa and causes the rivers flowing down to the coast to be broken by waterfalls and rapids. Men were unable, therefore, to reach the interior of Africa in the way they were able to reach the interior of North America; not only was the way guarded by these obstacles, it was further blocked by forests and mangrove swamps.

Of the four main obstacles to men's movements in the southern part of Africa which have been listed in the first paragraph, only one had been overcome by the end of the eighteenth century; and Swift's well-known verse

> So Geographers, in Afric maps,
> With savage pictures fill their gaps,
> And o'er uninhabitable downs,
> Place elephants for want of towns

still rang true, despite the great discoveries of the sixteenth and seventeenth centuries. These had merely revealed the coast of Africa to the people of Europe. The eastern side of this had, of course, long been known to the peoples of Asia. These peoples, however, had been halted by the lack of navigable rivers, a feature which is shown in Map 6. Nor had men found easy the long march up from the coast through the waterless land which stretched inland for many miles. The early traders, therefore, stayed on the coastal plain, where men died from fever.

First European contacts with Africans. Some knowledge of the interior was possessed by the Arab slavers, and the Portuguese had had consider-

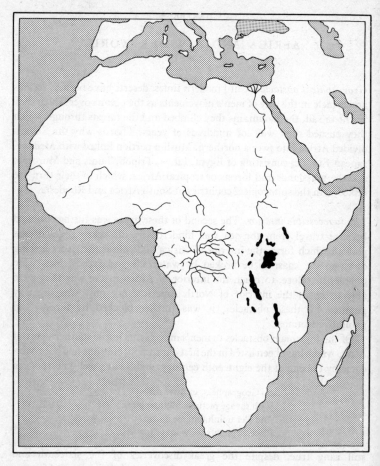

Map 6   The navigable stretches of waterways in Africa

able knowledge of parts of it; but there was no real contact between the
Africans and the peoples of either the East or the West until the
nineteenth century. It was then that the first vague outline of the
features of the interior became known to the peoples of Europe. They
had been known for centuries to the Africans who lived there, but travel
for these was still a slow matter, and very few had knowledge of any
large area. The coming of European explorers was to bring Africa into
touch with the peoples of the West. This was important, for it brought
the stimulus of new ideas to East Africa. It was also important for the

people of Europe, who were finding out about a continent that was to play a big part in world affairs in the twentieth century.

Everywhere the explorers went they came across trade with its tolls, market-places, tracks, and people who enjoyed singing, story-telling, dancing and drinking. The degree of organisation varied from that of nomad tribes to the well-run kingdom of Kimweri described on pages 39–40. Those for whom the explorers wrote were usually more interested in Africa itself than its peoples, till Livingstone's writings made his fellow-Europeans realise that Africans were human beings with faults and virtues, just like themselves. Europeans had for a very long time been fascinated by two mysteries in Africa: one, the source of the Nile; the other, the course of the Niger. Old charts show that Africa was one of the three continents which were known in ancient days. Yet, on closer examination it will be seen that the Nile is drawn as rising in very queer places, and it flows in impossible directions. It even sometimes joins the Niger.

The course of the Niger was the first of the two mysteries to be solved. In 1788 the African Association was founded to provide the money for expeditions to find out where the Niger went. In 1830 the mystery was finally solved by Richard Lander, who sailed down the Niger to its wide delta and found that it had long been familiar to Europeans under the name of the Oil River.

The problem of the Nile. In the second century A.D. there was a great Greek geographer called Ptolemy. In this time men knew that there were both a Blue and a White Nile, and it was Ptolemy's opinion that both the Niles had their source in lakes. The Blue Nile, he considered, rose in a lake in the east. The White, on the other hand, he thought, rose in large lakes which were fed by the Mountains of the Moon. This was the sort of information that sometimes trickled through from men who traded with the east coast of Africa; but for over 1,600 years the peoples of Europe knew no more about the source of the White Nile. It was a fascinating problem; and the first step to its solution was taken when, in 1770, the British explorer Bruce reached the source of the Blue Nile at Gheesh in Abyssinia, south of Lake Tana.

Krapf and Rebmann. In the middle of the nineteenth century, European interest was greatly increased by the discoveries of two German missionaries, Krapf (see above) and Rebmann, who established a mission station at Rabai. Malaria had already killed Krapf's wife and child, and throughout their work in East Africa both had to struggle with unknown diseases, master new languages, and explore the land sufficiently to

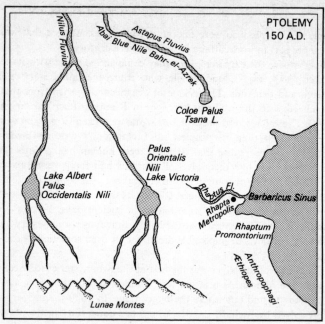

Map 7   Ptolemy's map and the 'Slug' map of 1855

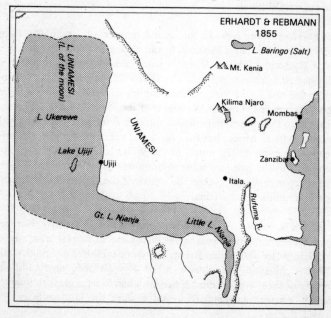

establish the chain of mission posts of which Krapf dreamt, as the bases from which Christianity could be spread throughout the interior. Soon after his arrival at Mombasa, in 1844, Krapf became very interested in the Kamba, who 'go in caravans of from 200–300 persons into the interior to fetch ivory, and form in a general way, the commercial medium between the coast and the interior, into which this journey is a distance of from 200–250 leagues'. He was already studying Swahili and noting down characteristics of the country on his short journeys round Mombasa. In 1847 he went into the Taita hills, about a hundred miles from Mombasa. It was in these hills that a pygmy people had probably lived, some 500 years earlier, before they were poisoned by later invaders, in whose history Rebmann was interested. He was the first European of whom we have record to go into the interior of East Africa, and he kept a careful account of his journeys. These provide contemporary written descriptions of East Africa, before the coming of Europeans on a large scale; and show that Africans, particularly the Kamba and the Chagga, were already playing an active part in developing trade.

First-hand evidence about the Kamba and Chagga 1847–8. As by 1847 many of the Taita tribe had spread to Taveta and the slopes of Kilimanjaro, where they mingled with the Chagga, Rebmann decided in the following year to follow up what he had heard about the Chagga people and the mountainous country in which they lived. On the way the country reminded him of Switzerland because it was so beautiful. 'Our way was across the bed of a mountain stream, over hill and dale, through plantations of Indian corn and beans, past small herds of cattle belonging to the Taita, then along fields of sugar, corn and banana.' He took with him some of the coastal Nyika, who wanted to know what his trading plans were, for the Chagga not only provisioned caravans, but traded with them. Ivory and slaves were usually bartered for lead amulets, beads and copper wire, which could be made into bracelets. At the time of Krapf's first visit the Chagga had only indirect contacts with Seyyid Said's commercial empire, which is described in Chapter 5. They had closer links with the coastal cities, which also had established monopolies; Pangani, for instance, completely controlled the products of the tribes on the banks of the river of the same name, getting from them rice, Indian corn, horned cattle, ivory, slaves, etc. Already Kilema was used as a stopping-place on the mountain, and once traders arrived at Kilimanjaro they found a route to the west over the plains for the caravans.

There was a fixed pattern for this trade in the interior, in which the

Kamba acted as middlemen and were the commercial link between the coast and the interior. They had an understanding with the Nyika at the coast, whereby each tribe was well treated by the other when in its area. Rebmann reported that the Kamba claimed to have come originally from the south-east direction of Chaggaland, and had then settled down to agriculture but kept in touch with the tribes with which they had been friendly. Most of the profitable ivory-trade was, in Rebmann's opinion, in their hands. This gave the Kamba the useful trading connections which enabled them to dominate the whole transport business to the coast in their area. Rebmann goes on to describe their customs. They marry on maturity, and their wives have to cultivate, grind corn, and to fetch wood and water, for which they use calabashes. Food mainly consists of milk and meat and a thick porridge made out of mealie-meal. In building their houses they use wooden stakes to make a circular wall, and thatch the roof with the fibres of barks of trees; bedsteads consist of wooden poles resting on two posts. He found that the Chagga, however, largely shared their dwellings with their cattle – this points to their pastoral origins – despite which they bathed so regularly that no one could call them dirty. Their buildings were always in isolated enclosures; nowhere in Chaggaland did he see a compact village or town.

Kivoi, a Kamba trader. Rebmann was also interested in systems of government; the Kamba he noticed had no kings or chiefs, and did not regard any laws as universally binding; rather they were ruled by the heads of the different family villages, who followed old customs and the usage of the country. 'Wealth, a ready flow of language, an imposing personal appearance and above all the reputation of being a magician and rain-maker are means by which an Akamba can attain power and importance and secure the obedience of his countrymen.' Kivoi possessed all these qualities in a high degree; hence his great influence in Ukambani. He was also an outstanding trader among a people noted for their activities in this field, and told Rebmann that there was a need for river transport from Mombasa as the country was so difficult. It was when staying in Kamba country, at Kitui, that Krapf caught a glimpse of Mount Kenya and told the chief how much he would like to go beyond the River Tana to the country in which the mountain was to be found. Much to Kivoi's surprise, in 1850 Krapf managed to get inland and join him for part of a trip. Kivoi was planning this with the object of getting ivory near Kilema and selling it at the coast. On the way the party was attacked by robbers, Kivoi was killed and his followers scattered; Krapf, however, struggled on and 'In Mberre land, on the other side of the river, I saw a lofty mountain.' In his book, *Travels, Researches and Missionary*

Labours he described East Africa's two major peaks, Mounts Kiliman-jaro and Kenya.

The truth is not believed. In England Krapf's account of his travels aroused considerable interest, and the Royal Geographical Society commissioned Richard Burton to investigate reports, which included the statement that there existed a lake of sweet water, 800 miles long by 300 miles broad; its position was indicated in the 'slug map' of Erhardt

Fig. 4   Rabbai Mpia – a sketch from a book by Krapf

and Rebmann (see Map 7). It seemed very unlikely, but possibly not more improbable than Rebmann's report in 1849 that there was a snow-covered mountain called Kilimanjaro in East Africa. W. D. Cooley, a member of the newly-founded Royal Geographical Society, poured scorn on the idea: 'The only true explanation of it is contained in Mr. Rebmann's confession that he is very short-sighted.' When Rebmann endeavoured to explain his discovery to his comparatively sharp-sighted attendants, they seemed unwilling 'to trust his words at once'. Cooley had not realised the passionate interest which Krapf and Rebmann had in scientific accuracy, which make their reports a useful source of information about Kenya before the colonial era began. Burton was another explorer whose colourful descriptions add to our knowledge of life in East Africa over a hundred years ago.

Zanzibar. Burton visited Zanzibar at the end of the reign of Seyyid Said, of whom you have read in Chapter 2, and reported that:

> In 1835 Dr. Ruschauberger estimated the census of Zanzibar at 12,000 souls, of whom two-thirds were slaves. In 1844 Dr. Krapf proposed 100,000 as the population of the island, the greater number living in the capital. Dr. Guillain, in 1846, gave 20,000 to 25,000, slaves included. I assumed the number in 1857, as 25,000, which during the N.E. monsoon, when a large floating population flocks in, may rise to 40,000 and even to 45,000. The consular report of 1849 asserts it to be about 60,000.
>
> The city is divided into 18 quarters (Mahallat) each having its own name. The west-end boasts the best houses, chiefly those which wealthy natives let to stranger merchants. The Central, or Fort Quarter is the seat of government and commerce, whilst few foreigners inhabit the eastern extremities, the hottest and the most unhealthy. The streets are, as they should be under such a sky, deep and winding alleys, hardly 20 feet broad, and travellers compare them with the threads of a tangled skein.

The Nyamwezi. In 1856 Burton, accompanied by Speke, set out to investigate the mystery of the great lake described above. Starting from Zanzibar, he passed through the richly cultivated fields of Unyamwezi, where he saw 'a hall which was usually full of buyers and sellers, Arab and African, and large investments of wire beads and cotton cloths, some of them valuable, are regularly sent from the coast'. He found

> The African in these regions superior in comforts, better dressed, fed and lodged and less worked than the unhappy ryot of British India. [Burton had travelled extensively; he had once made a daring journey to Mecca in disguise, and both he and Speke had been Indian Army Officers.] His condition where the slave-trade is slack may indeed be compared advantageously with that of the peasantry in some of the richest European countries.

He also commented that the Nyamwezi 'have a passion for gambling, and live on meat when they can, but the daily food of the poor is grain'. It is tempting to wonder if love of gambling was linked with a readiness to take a lead in the developing gamble of trade. The prizes could be rich. Burton in his book, *The Lake Regions of Central Africa*, tells of Musa Mzuri going back to Zanzibar with a load of ivory worth £7,500. By the second half of the nineteenth century Arab traders were supplanting the Nyamwezi, who remained, however, in great demand as porters. To quote Burton again: 'The Nyamwezi bear the highest character for civilization, discipline and industry.' Taking part in a caravan was considered by them to be a profitable experience which it was worth even a chief's while to secure; Mirambo's career is an example of this.

Victoria Nyanza and the source of the Nile. As Burton and Speke drew nearer to Lake Tanganyika they found, by conversation with the Arabs, that the great lake they were seeking was really three lakes, great distances apart, and that the tales Krapf and Rebmann had heard referred to Lake Tanganyika, Lake Nyasa, and the largest lake of all, later named Victoria. Despite the help they had received from the Arabs in the way of transport, supplies and information, the journey had proved a great strain. Burton was so broken-down in health that he let Speke go on alone in the direction of Victoria Nyanza. When Speke reported the existence of the giant lake Burton denied that it could be the long-sought source of the Nile. On coming back to England Speke was commissioned by the Royal Geographical Society to return to Africa, to trace the link between the lake and the Nile. In 1862 he became the first European to enter Buganda. It was then that he wrote the description on page 44 of the court of the kabaka, before going on to Bunyoro. Despite Burton's contempt for Speke's gifts as a cartographer – he said Speke 'could not grasp and did not see the importance of grasping a fact, and his vagueness of thought necessarily extended to his language' – the outline of the interlacustrine area was becoming increasingly clear. Armed with Speke's map, another explorer, Baker, reached Lake Albert and the Murchison Falls, but the whole Nile system was not accurately mapped until Stanley paid a visit to the area several years later. Previously the Africans who lived there had known the features of the local landscape, and traders had a working knowledge of routes, but they had not got an accurate map of East Africa as a whole. Puzzling this out was not easy, because the explorers, as we have seen, did not always agree among themselves. It was, however, necessary to have accurate maps if Africa was to become part of the world's communication system.

Livingstone. Mungo Park, Speke, Burton, Grant and Baker were all geographers and naturalists, whose interests were in scientific exploration; but Krapf and Rebmann had shown the close link that could exist between the spreading of Christianity and the discovery of more information about the unknown continent. The greatest explorer of all was a medical missionary, David Livingstone.

By the time he was ten, David Livingstone had shown great determination. As there was no money to educate him, he went to work for fourteen hours a day in a cotton mill, but that did not mean that he gave

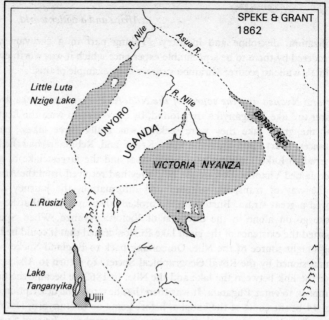

Map 8   Speke's map of 1862 and Stanley's map of 1877

up hope of learning. He bought a Latin Grammar with his first week's wages and studied after working hours. In this way he qualified himself to be accepted by the London Missionary Society; and while waiting to be posted abroad he studied medicine and became a doctor. He went to his first post in Bechuanaland in 1841 and there met the Makololo people. It was through his good relations with these that he became the first European to see the mighty river Zambezi. He also learnt that the Makololo had recently combined with another tribe to raid for slaves to exchange for guns with the Arabs. From that time Livingstone fought hard against the slave-trade and its supporters. As he said, prominent slave-dealers were 'the Banians [who] have the Custom House and all the public revenue of Zanzibar entirely in their hands and by their money, arms, ammunitions and goods a large and cruel slave-trade has been carried on. They would not hurt a flea or murder but they are virtually the worst cannibals in all Africa.' In order to combat slavery Livingstone was convinced that a positive policy was needed. He thought it was necessary to establish a mission station which should also be a centre for farmers and traders; for in his opinion the greatest obstacle to the spread of Christianity among the Africans was the poverty and ignorance and fear which surrounded them. If they were to be freed from this they would have to be introduced to a higher standard of living and shown that it was possible for the different tribes to work together, thus increasing their power to resist violence.

First expedition. In those days a settlement of the nature Livingstone had in mind depended on climate and communications. In searching for this Livingstone set out on the first of his three great journeys. This lasted from 1853 to 1856 and took him right across Africa, from Barotseland to the Atlantic Ocean at Loanda, and then back to reach the sea on the east coast at Quelimane. For a large part of this journey he had followed the course of the Zambezi, and in doing so he had, in 1855, seen the Victoria Falls. Now he wondered whether this river would not be a better means of communication than any land route.

Appeal to Cambridge. On his return to England he found himself famous through the publication of his book *Missionary Travels and Researches*; and he used his fame to appeal to Cambridge University for help in carrying on the work he had begun in opening the way for commerce and Christianity in Africa. The result was the foundation of the Universities Mission to Central Africa. He also secured government support for his second important expedition, the object of which was to explore the

Zambezi valley up from the mouth of the river in the hope that it might prove a good means of communication.

Second expedition. This second expedition lasted from 1858 to 1864 and resulted in Europe hearing of the existence of Lakes Shirwa and Nyasa and eventually in the establishment of mission stations, followed by traders, and the declaration of the protectorate of Nyasaland.

Object of third expedition. Livingstone set out on his third important journey in 1866. This was to be his last. Its object was geographical: Speke and Baker had reported their discoveries, but Burton and some other maintained that their theories of the source of the Nile were incorrect, or at least incomplete. Besides, no one yet knew where the central watershed lay. The president of the Royal Geographical Society suggested that Livingstone might be able to settle the question by going from the upper Rovuma to Lake Tanganyika and then exploring westwards. This would give him a chance to see if the Nile not only flowed out of Lakes Victoria and Albert in the north, as Speke and Baker had shown, but first flowed into the southern end of these lakes. If this idea should prove correct, the true source might be Lake Tanganyika. Livingstone was far from convinced that Speke and Baker were right, and was delighted at the opportunity of exploring these possibilities. He at once agreed, provided he was allowed also to use every opportunity to fight against the slave-trade and to spread Christianity.

Results. In view of these plans, Livingstone decided to operate from two bases. In the first, Zanzibar, he planned to recruit porters, obtain supplies and arrange for reinforcements. The second base was to be Ujiji, on Lake Tanganyika. From here Livingstone meant to explore the land around, looking for the Nile and endeavouring to identify the central watershed. Although it was far to the south of his goal, the true Nile sources, Livingstone's last journey was not unproductive. He saw Lake Bangweulu in 1868, and was exploring the Lualaba, or upper reaches of the Congo when he died, in 1873.

Achievements. It is not easy to sum up Livingstone's achievements: he carried on Wilberforce's work for the abolition of slavery, enlisting the sympathy of the British for the Africans by making Africa real to them through his letters and books. As an explorer he changed the maps of Africa. Lastly, it was through his work that Nyasaland eventually became a part of the British Commonwealth. Today his reputation still stands high, as an utterly fearless man, serving the highest ideals, and

THE EUROPEAN TAKE-OVER

Missionaries, abolitionists, explorers and traders from Europe and America had been interested in East Africa for many years before the 1880s, but politicians had generally avoided getting involved with it. Let East Africa develop by the encouragement of Christianity and commerce, but leave the administration to the sultan and local rulers – such was the British policy, and no one seriously challenged it. But in the 1880s the politicians of Europe began to take an interest in Africa and policies had perforce to change.

East Africa was only one of the areas which was involved. One might start the main story with Leopold of the Belgians and his international African Association which, as we have seen, began in 1876. Having failed to find a satisfactory approach to the interior of the continent from the east, he sent Stanley to explore the approach from the west by way of the Congo, in 1879. The French had also sent an expedition there under De Brazza, and both explorers claimed the area. To add to the complications, Portugal also revived her ancient claims to the Congo mouth, and in order to gain Portuguese support in abolishing the slave-trade in that area Britain recognised her claims in 1884. Both Leopold and the French objected.

Germany, Bismarck and the Berlin Conference (1884–5). It was at this point that Germany, led by Bismarck, invited all the European countries concerned to a conference in Berlin, to discuss the future of the Congo in particular and the partition of African territories in general.

Germany, which had long been a patchwork of semi-independent states, had united in 1870 under the leadership of the state of Prussia, and had embarked on a successful policy of conquest and consolidation. The real brain behind this united Germany was the German chancellor, Bismarck, and for him it was the politics of Europe which were always the main consideration. He believed – as Britain did – that colonies were expensive burdens, and at first he opposed them, but in 1884 he began to see that they might be used as useful political levers. For one thing there was enthusiasm for them in Germany, so that his support for colonisation would strengthen his position in the German Reichstag. Moreover, by careful choice of support in rival colonial claims he might

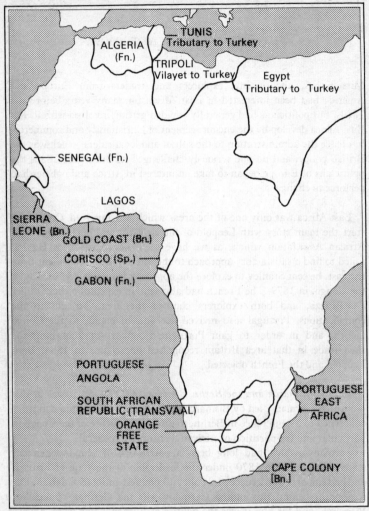

ALGERIA
(Fn.)

TUNIS
Tributary to Turkey

TRIPOLI
Vilayet to Turkey

Egypt
Tributary to Turkey

SENEGAL (Fn.)

LAGOS

SIERRA
LEONE (Bn.)

GOLD COAST (Bn.)

CORISCO (Sp.)

GABON (Fn.)

PORTUGUESE
ANGOLA

SOUTH AFRICAN
REPUBLIC (TRANSVAAL)

ORANGE
FREE
STATE

PORTUGUESE
EAST
AFRICA

CAPE COLONY
(Bn.)

Map 12   Lands controlled by Europeans in Africa in 1876

increase French hostility to Britain while reducing it towards Germany. Therefore, in 1884, Bismarck became interested in African colonisation, and the Berlin Conference was called at his suggestion.

It was willingly attended, and its decisions were stated in the Berlin Act of 1885. So far as the Congo was concerned, Leopold was recognised as sovereign of the new Congo Independent State although the 'conventional Congo basin' was to be an area under international protection with trade open to all. Bismarck tried to restrict British claims by insisting that protectorates could only be recognised if they were effectively managed. The British forced him to reduce this to merely informing other countries of new claims, and in East Africa it was the Germans who in fact used this to their advantage.

From 1884 the whole process of partition accelerated. The Germans laid claims in West, South-west, and East Africa. The French pushed southwards from Algiers and westwards from Senegal, establishing an enormous area of influence across northern Africa and the northern Congo, besides occupying Madagascar in the east. Cecil Rhodes, dreaming of an Africa which he hoped would be British from the Cape to Cairo, extended British influence northwards to Bechuanaland and the Rhodesias, thus driving a wedge between the Portuguese territory of Mozambique on the east and Angola on the west. Meanwhile the Italians maintained their hold on Eritrea and established a protectorate over the whole Somali coast.

In East Africa the fears of the Sultan and Sir John Kirk suddenly became a reality as three young Germans led by Carl Peters and disguised as mechanics, landed in Zanzibar and went over to the mainland to stake out a claim to the southern portion which they maintained for over thirty years.

German interests. These three young men were not the first Germans to show an interest in colonies and East Africa. The German Society for the Scientific Exploration of Equatorial Africa had been started in 1873 and others had followed, with the keen support of German traders. The explorers, Dr Nachtigal, Dr Rohlfs and Dr Schweinfurth and the Denhardt brothers, were Germans. But all these had met with Bismarck's refusal to accept colonisation.

Carl Peters was neither great nor good. His university education left him with a vision limited to nationalism and a nature which was both cruel and deceitful. On the other hand he had huge determination, and having decided that Germany needed colonies he set off with two friends in 1884, landed at Zanzibar in November, and then spent about a fortnight on the mainland travelling up and down the Wami River making treaties with chiefs, to whom his papers meant nothing at all. A typical example is:

Treaty of eternal friendship: Mangungo, Sultan of Msovero in Usangara, offers all his territory with all its civil and public appurtenances to Dr Carl Peters as the representative of the Society for German Colonisation, for exclusive and universal utilisation for German colonisation.

By December Peters was back in Zanzibar, and by February 1885 he was back in Berlin. Moreover Bismarck had just changed his mind and decided to support colonisation. The treaties which Peters had made were therefore recognised by the German government, which formally announced in March that Usagara was annexed. Meanwhile the Denhardt brothers had visited the northern area of the coast and after negotiating with the rebel, Simba, in Witu they announced in April that this also was a German protectorate. This meant that the Germans now claimed the south and a strategic area of the north. If only these regions could be joined by getting the area to the west of the British sphere then German claims would encircle those of Britain.

The annexation of Usagara and Witu, 1885. The claims of Germany had huge results. The sultan himself was indignant, and sent a note of protest to the German emperor. 'These territories are ours', he wrote, 'and we hold military stations there [at Usagara], and those chiefs who profess to cede sovereign rights have no authority to do so.' For support he looked to Britain, and at this point it became clear that the British policy of controlling East Africa through the sultan was over.

The truth was that the British government was no longer as interested in the area now that the slave-trade had been effectively ended. Moreover they were facing an unusual number of bigger troubles at the same time, since in January General Gordon had been murdered in Khartoum, as the Mahdist revolt gathered strength in the Sudan, and in March the Russians began to advance into Afghanistan. The British government considered these threats in North Africa and India much more important than East Africa and were quite clear that they did not wish to make an enemy of the Germans. Therefore Gladstone, the British prime minister, said, 'If Germany becomes a colonising power, all I can say is "God speed her".'

The sultan and John Kirk felt that they had been let down, and in August the Germans, realising the British attitude, sent to Zanzibar a naval squadron which offered the sultan the choice of accepting the treaties made by Germany with the sultans of Usagara, Nguru, Useguha, Ukami and Witu, or else having Zanzibar blown to bits. The sultan accepted the treaties and the annexation became official.

The Zanzibar Commission, 1885–6. The next question was, what exactly were the limits of the sultan's territories? The Germans had disregarded his rights in some areas but they did not deny them altogether, and the most critical area was the coastal one, which lay between their claims and their means of reaching them by sea. To settle

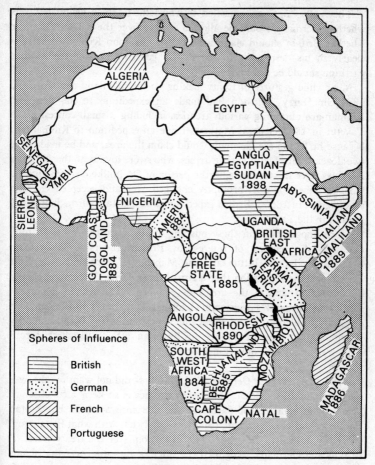

Map 13   The partition of Africa 1879–1899

this the British persuaded the Germans and French to form a commission, which duly inspected the coast. Officially it decided very little, except that the main islands and ports were definitely in the sultan's dominions, but in any case it could not claim to be fair or representative when the sultan was not included. Perhaps the most interesting outcome of it all was the remark in the official despatch suggesting the crucial importance of Mombasa as the best commercial base for opening the interior.

The really important question to which the German claims led, was whether Germany would be allowed to take over the whole region, or whether Britain should claim a part of it. Sir John Kirk put this very clearly in his despatches to the British government and argued that partition should be demanded.

Meanwhile gestures of treaty-making on the mainland continued. In 1884 Sir Harry Johnston had made an expedition to the slopes of Kilimanjaro obtaining various treaties, including a small concession at Taveta; in 1885 General Mathews made an expedition to Kilimanjaro because he feared the Germans would claim the area, and he made over two dozen treaties with various tribes, who swore loyalty to the sultan; a few days later the Germans, in the person of Dr Juhlke, arrived and the Chagga tribe, for one, promptly changed over and accepted German sovereignty; in 1866 a British expedition was sent to confirm Johnston's treaties in the Taveta area.

More important than these bustling affairs were two other factors. One was the renewal of interest by British traders – Sir William Mackinnon, James Hutton and the Manchester merchants – in East Africa, and the suggestion that a British East Africa Association should be formed to control the area's development. The second important factor was Bismarck's decision in October 1886 to finish off the Zanzibar negotiations before the claims became too extensive and bothersome. By threatening to support France in Egyptian affairs Bismarck forced Britain to an agreement within a fortnight.

The partition treaty of October 1886. Bismarck did not want to take over the whole of East Africa. He was by no means so keen a coloniser as Peters. The principle of partition was therefore accepted but Sultan Barghash was not represented and was simply left with what Britain and Germany agreed to recognise. The main points of the treaty were: (i) Britain and Germany recognised the sultan's authority over the islands of Zanzibar, Pemba, Mafia and Lamu, and also over the coast, to a depth of 10 miles from the River Rovuma in the south to Kipini in the north. North of that the towns of Kismayu, Barawa, Merka, Mogadishu and Warsheikh were also recognised as the sultan's. (ii) The territory between the Rivers Rovuma and Tana was to be divided into German and British spheres of influence by the line which now marks the boundary between Kenya and Tanzania. (iii) Britain agreed to support Germany's claim to establishing a custom's-house at Dar es Salaam. Dar es Salaam thus virtually became a German possession leased from the sultan. (iv) Britain agreed to recognise the German possession of Witu and its corridor to the sea at Manda Bay.

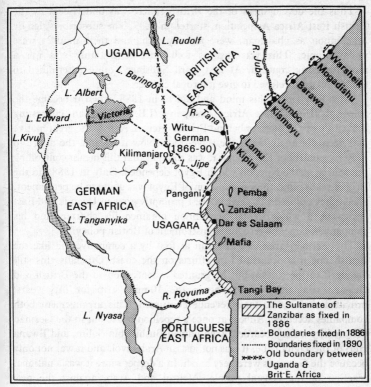

Map 14   The Anglo-German agreements of 1886 and 1890

Although the treaty ended the probability of Germany taking over the whole coast, it certainly did not settle the partition of East Africa. The western boundaries were not defined and claims and counter-claims continued to be made, as we shall see.

The rival companies. Meanwhile the British government, now led by Lord Salisbury, had no intention of taking any more steps in East Africa if it could be avoided. The object of the treaty had been to keep the Germans out of at least a part of East Africa but the prime minister shuddered at the idea of getting further involved, and would not even agree to sending an expedition to rescue Emin Pasha from Equatoria; so Sir William Mackinnon had to organise it privately – he sent Stanley who, with his formidable efficiency, completed the task in 1889.

Thus the development of the British sphere was undertaken by the British East Africa Association, started in 1887. The subscribers, led by Mackinnon as chairman, were already rich, and their motives were philanthropic. This was just as well since it certainly was not a money-making concern. At first Lord Salisbury, quite determined to remain neutral, refused to give it a royal charter.

That he changed his mind and did so in 1888, when it became the Imperial British East Africa Company (I.B.E.A.), is an interesting indication of the motives behind British interest. At first the great motive had been the abolition of the slave-trade. Now it became the desire to preserve control of Egypt, and it was thought that this meant controlling the source of the Nile, on which Egypt depended. Only in 1888 did the British realise that their occupation of Egypt was going to be permanent. When they realised this their interest promptly grew in Uganda and East Africa as a whole. Thus Mackinnon obtained his charter, and his company became the recognised instrument of British policy.

The German area was also run at first by a company, and like the British one it concentrated its efforts on the coast. Officially this still belonged to the sultan, but he granted a concession to the British and German companies to administer the 10-mile strip for fifty years, provided that his customs revenue continued. This arrangement both companies accepted. Almost at once a rebellion broke out in the German belt, led by a fiery bearded Arab named Bushiri bin Salim, and Bwana Heri of the Zigua tribe. It was not just an Arab revolt and it was not only because the Germans were very harsh. In a deeper sense it was a national reaction of the coastal people, African and Arab, against the new invaders. The British realised this and co-operated with the Germans to end the revolt. The German government realised the position also and decided that the time had come to take over the company's affairs. Meanwhile the company had been driven from most of the coastal towns, and so General Wissman was sent to restore order with a force of Sudanese, Zulu and Somali troops in 1889. Throughout that year the rebellion went on, until in December Bagamoyo was taken and Bushiri was hanged. Bwana Heri submitted the following April. But for all Europeans in East Africa it was a time of bitter feeling, and a general attack upon them was feared in Zanzibar.

Although the British helped the German company to restore order, in other ways there was considerable rivalry. Much of it came from the German Witu company in the north, which put in one claim after another for Lamu, for the territory between Witu and Juba, and for the islands of Manda and Patta. These were rejected by an international committee, but Witu still remained a source of trouble.

Peters realised this. He realised too that no agreement had been made about whose sphere of influence Uganda should become, and he wanted it to be German so that the British sphere would be encircled. As a pretext, but only as a pretext, he therefore announced that he was leading a German expedition to relieve Emin Pasha. Despite the fact that Stanley had already left for this, despite the fact that Bushiri's rebellion was in full swing, despite Wissman's refusal to recognise his authority, and despite the British patrol vessels, Peters still landed at Witu in July 1889 and set off up the Tana with 300 men. A month later the British company replied by sending an experienced hunter, Mr (later Sir) Frederick Jackson, to explore towards Lake Victoria as well. Jackson reached Uganda first, but having been forbidden by the company to get involved in Uganda's politics he went on an elephant shoot to help pay for his expedition. While this gentlemanly sport was going on Peters arrived, and persuaded the kabaka to sign a treaty placing Uganda under German protection. Then he went back to Bagamoyo. Jackson, when he returned to Uganda, was infuriated by the action of Peters. Peters, when he returned to Bagamoyo, was infuriated by the action of the German government who, in his absence, had agreed to recognise Uganda as a British sphere.

The Heligoland Treaty, 1890. Lord Salisbury, with his concern for the Nile and Egypt, was worried when he heard a rumour that Wissman was to move to Uganda, followed by the news of Peters' treaty with the kabaka. He therefore offered the island of Heligoland in the North Sea to the Germans as a naval base provided that they would make concessions in East Africa in return. The offer tempted the Germans towards a speedy settlement, and after Bismark had ceased to be chancellor in March 1890 negotiations moved quickly towards agreement.

From the British point of view three things were desirable: (i) That a British protectorate should be recognised over Zanzibar, where German influence had grown at such an alarming rate – Wissman had made it the headquarters of the German company and the German residents there outnumbered other European residents by six to one. The sultan was very ready to accept a British protectorate for he feared that the Germans would soon overshadow his own authority there. (ii) That the western frontiers of the German and British spheres should be continued westwards to Lake Victoria and across it to the boundary of the Congo Free State, so that Uganda should be included in the British area. (iii) That the Germans should abandon all claims to regions north of the British sphere, which would mean the end of the Witu protectorate.

The Germans on their side were willing to agree to this in return for two main concessions: (i) That the British should help to persuade the sultan to cede absolutely to Germany the ten-mile strip of the mainland which had been held on lease since the 1886 agreement. The sultan, with some reluctance, agreed to this in return for compensation equivalent to £200,000. (ii) That the island of Heligoland in the North Sea should be given to Germany by Britain. The Germans believed that this would be a valuable naval base, although the future was to show that it was not.

Such was the 1890 agreement, which ended the scramble so far as East Africa was concerned. Even the claims of Italy and France were settled. The French objected at first to the agreement on the grounds that the 1862 declaration recognising the sultan's independence had been ignored, but they withdrew their objections when the British agreed to recognise their claims to a protectorate over Madagascar. The Italians had claimed Ethiopia and the northern ports on the East African coast. The British company agreed to a joint administration of the port of Kismayu, and in 1891 they recognised the Italian claims to the north. However, they defined the boundaries carefully, except in the north-western corner, and stipulated that no building should occur on the Nile tributaries in the Italian sphere which might alter the level of the river in Egypt.

The political battle was over, but the problems of development had hardly begun.

UGANDA

The region of Uganda, which had become a British sphere by the Heligoland Treaty, was passing through troubled times.

Religion and politics had become thoroughly mixed up. The Roman Catholic missionaries were French, and they were anxious to see French influence develop in Uganda; the Protestant missionaries were British; and in addition to the two Christian missions there were also the Arabs, who were Muslims and wanted to see a Muslim–Arab state. Even under the strong Kabaka Mutesa tensions ran high among these groups, and the kabaka wondered exactly what each wanted and exactly what each was prepared to offer; but because he was strong, no group became over-powerful, and the two Christian missions pursued their teaching with remarkable success. Father Lourdel baptised the first of his converts in 1880 and Mackay baptised his in 1882. Mackay also produced the first Luganda translations of the New Testament and began to teach people to read. Soon both Catholic and Protestant missions had more 'readers' than they could manage.

The Kabaka Mwanga. In 1884 Mutesa died and his successor was faced with problems which would have puzzled a genius. Mwanga was not a genius. He was overwhelmed by the situation which he found and his exasperated attempts to break through it only made things worse. As the kabaka's power weakened that of the rival groups increased, so that chiefs allied themselves where advantage seemed most likely.

Mwanga had been one of Mackay's 'readers', but on his accession he promptly became a Muslim, to the delight of the Arab party. He followed this by growing persecution of the Christians, which was partly caused by fear that they wanted to take over his country. This was understandable, in view of Joseph Thomson's expedition in 1883 to the northern end of Lake Victoria by the direct route from Mombasa, and the expedition of Carl Peters annexing Usagara. When Mwanga heard that Bishop Hannington was following Thomson's route to take up his appointment as bishop of eastern Equatorial Africa, in 1885, he arranged for him to be murdered. This was followed, in 1886, by burning alive about 30 Protestant and Catholic 'readers' in one ghastly bonfire, plus about 200 others around the capital. Despite this the Christian missions continued to flourish.

By 1888 Mwanga had become exasperated with the Muslim–Arab party as well as with the Christian ones, and he attempted to get rid of all three by marooning them on an island in Lake Victoria, while he turned for support to the traditional followers of Lubaalism. In fact, the Muslim and Christian parties combined to drive out Mwanga, and make his brother, Kiwewa, the kabaka. Revolution is a slippery slope, however, and at this point the Arab party made a successful attempt to gain complete control of the country. Christian missionaries and chiefs were driven out, taking refuge in Ankole, and when Kiwewa himself showed signs of opposition to the Arab leaders they promptly deposed him, and put his younger brother, Kalema, in his place.

The Arab take-over was serious, but short. During 1889 Mwanga reappeared and supported by some of the missionaries (mainly Catholic), plus the Christian refugees from Ankole led by Apolo Kagwa, his troops defeated the Arab party. This was in October, and Mwanga triumphantly built himself a new capital at Mengo. A month later the Arabs pushed him out again, helped by King Kabarega of Bunyoro, and it was not until the February of 1890 that the Arab–Muslim party was decisively defeated at Bulwanyi, so that Mwanga could settle down again as kabaka. Naturally he was now strongly anti-Arab and strongly pro-Catholic, as Father Lourdel had been much more helpful to him than the Protestant missions, and there were many more Catholic chiefs than Protestant ones.

Uganda becomes a protectorate. It was during this struggle that the Heligoland Treaty was negotiated, following the expeditions of Stanley, Jackson and Peters. They were not the only expeditions destined for Uganda at this period. The Imperial British East Africa Company was also planning to send a caravan inland, led by Captain (later Lord) Lugard. He was a remarkable young soldier, who had seen active service in India, the Sudan and Burma, and then tried to drown the sorrow of a broken love-affair by fighting slavers in Nyasaland. His startling courage and personality marked him out, and although I.B.E.A. did not realise that he was destined to become the greatest colonial administrator of his time they did realise that they were lucky to secure his services.

In August 1890 he set out from Mombasa. He paused for a while at Dagoretti on the edge of Kikuyu country, hoping for reinforcements which did not come, and then he plunged on again, reaching Uganda in December. As the company respresentative he was supposed to get the Kabaka Mwanga to recognise his controlling authority in return for the company's protection. After some hesitation Mwanga agreed; but the real question was whether the company could offer any protection and make its authority felt.

The political–religious groups were still hostile. The Catholic-French (Fransa) party were the most numerous, and they wished to revoke the agreement they had made with the Anglo-Protestant (Inglesa) party that chiefs who changed from one side to the other could not still claim their lands. The Inglesa party realised that any transfer of land would weaken their position, because they were the smaller group, and therefore they insisted on the agreement. Feelings ran high. Mwanga openly favoured the Catholics; Lugard was expected to favour the Protestants.

He started by building a fort on Kampala Hill and then united both Christian parties in another attack on the Muslims, who still threatened from Bunyoro. This was a good rallying-cry, and in May 1891 the Muslims were again defeated, whereupon Lugard set off westwards to enlist the help of Sudanese troops who had been left at Kavalli's, during Stanley's expedition to get Emin Pasha. Some of these Sudanese troops were used to garrison the Toro–Bunyoro border against the Muslims. The rest came back to Kampala to reinforce Lugard's tiny force.

They arrived on the last day of 1891, and in January 1892 the expected fighting broke out between the Fransa and Inglesa parties. Lugard had realised this was coming and had armed the Inglesa, but it was his Maxim gun which was really decisive and forced Mwanga and the Fransa chiefs to flee. At the end of March they returned, and by an agreement made between the Christian parties Uganda was re-divided. The Catholic chiefs were allocated the province of Buddu, and the Protestant chiefs were allocated the rest, except for three small counties lying between the two parties. These counties were given to the Muslims. Mwanga and all the chiefs agreed to accept the company's authority.

The proposal to withdraw. Meanwhile the company could not afford to continue administering Uganda, and Sir William Mackinnon informed the British government they would have to withdraw. The government were reluctantly prepared to accept this, but the British public were not. In September 1891 the leading article in *The Times* expressed the general feeling:

> Such a withdrawal would be nothing short of a national calamity. It would mean not only the loss of a great amount of capital already expended, but the destruction of our influence and prestige throughout Central Africa, the practical defeat of our anti-slavery policy, the persecution of the numerous missionaries labouring in Uganda, and the reconquest by Mohammedan fanatics of the only African state that has shown a disposition to accept Christianity. Whether we desire it or not, the British East Africa Company must be identified for all practical purposes with national policy.

While the government reconsidered its decision, in view of popular feeling, Mackinnon and his friends subscribed a further £25,000 and Bishop Tucker raised £15,000, by an appeal to the C.M.S. Gleaners Union. This enabled the company to remain in Uganda for another year, and in 1892 Lugard himself returned and added his own persuasions. As a result the government agreed to send Sir Gerald Portal, the consul-general of Zanzibar, to visit Uganda and make a report, while the company was to be given financial aid to enable it to continue its occupation until March 1893.

Uganda becomes a protectorate, 1894. The verdict of Portal was a foregone conclusion, because the main facts of the situation were well known in Zanzibar. On 1 April 1893, soon after his arrival, he hauled down the company's flag on Kampala Hill, replaced it with the Union Jack, and proclaimed a provisional British protectorate over the region. He also made a new agreement with Mwanga, and also with the Catholic chiefs, adding the province of Kamia and the island of Sese to Buddu. In his official report to the government, Portal emphasised again the need to protect the missionaries, the promise to end slave-trading in the interior, and the strategic importance of Uganda in controlling the headwaters of the Nile. After much opposition parliament confirmed the protectorate, in August 1894.

The British East African protectorate, 1895. When the British govern-ment took over Uganda as a protectorate the company's responsibilities there ended, and automatically its position in the rest of East Africa was questioned too.

Its position had always been impossible because its capital was completely inadequate and its revenue almost non-existent, so it was just as well that those who subscribed to it acted from philanthropic motives. Nevertheless it had some significant achievements to its credit, not least the intervention in Uganda which had wrecked its finances.

Elsewhere it had explored the possibilities of the Tana and Juba Rivers as trade-routes to the interior, without much success, and Mackinnon, at his own expense, had built a road across the Taru plain – the grim, dry scrubland lying behind the coastal palms. At the inland base of Machakos an industrial training-centre for Africans had been started. Generally, however, the company's relations with the people on the coast were spoilt, because the company was expected to enforce anti-slavery laws, although slavery was an institution on which the coastal society to a great extent depended. Thus the company was too weak and inefficient to make a strong, effective impression, but it constituted a threat to the whole way of life of the coastal peoples.

When Uganda became a protectorate, and as the last trickle of revenue disappeared in 1892, when the British government imposed free trade on the coast, the directors began negotiations with the government to end the company. They were given an ungenerous compensation of £250,000 for their services, and on 15 June 1895 their remaining territories were taken over by the foreign office as the British East Africa protectorate.

CHAPTER 8

EARLY COLONIAL EXPERIMENTS, 1890–1918

We have seen in Chapter 7 that the British government took over direct control of Zanzibar in 1890, of Uganda in 1894 and of the British East Africa protectorate in 1895, while the German government took over direct control of its protectorate in 1891.

How on earth were these colossal areas to be administered and developed?

One idea was to govern through existing authorities, and this theory was called 'indirect rule'. The great trouble about it was that in most of the areas effective authorities did not exist, and where they did – as in Zanzibar and Uganda – they were not sufficiently strong or efficient to exist without support.

It was also necessary to make the protectorates pay their way, by encouraging production and communications. This meant that railways had to be built and commercial crops had to be found to replace subsistence farming.

The question of who was to grow the crops then arose. Should it be the African people or was it necessary to bring in settlers with specialised farming skills and capital?

How was the ownership of land to be decided? Where was the labour for farming and other enterprises, like road-building, to come from? How was the money to be raised to pay for administration in regions where there was practically no money, and where the people already grew the food they needed, and required practically nothing else?

The answers to these questions were not always the expected ones. For example, at the outset Zanzibar was the main East African base, and the protectorates behind were regarded, in the words of historian Bethwell Ogot, as a 'kind of Zanzibar backyard', but within two decades this position was completely reversed. Similarly, although most of the administrators thought that the only way to make the Uganda railway pay was to encourage European settlers, it turned out that the most profitable early farming came from the African cotton-growers.

In fact the story of the early colonial period is one of military conquest by expeditions against those who refused to accept the intruders; it is mixed with diplomatic encouragement of key people and tribes who were willing to co-operate; it is a story of trial and error, where the men on the spot often took things into their own hands, sometimes for better, sometimes for worse.

But the outcome of it all was that the East African scene had radically changed. Tribal warfare had ended, although tribal feeling had not, and this newly-found peace, coupled with the railways and roads made possible the flow of trade and ideas with the outside world.

Let us now see how the problems were faced in each protectorate.

ZANZIBAR

The establishment of British control. Seyyid Barghash died in 1888, to be succeeded by Seyyid Khalifa (1888–90) and Seyyid Ali (1890–3).

When the British protectorate over Zanzibar was declared, in November 1890, it was generally welcomed by the sultan and the Arab court. To them it seemed they had much to gain by leaving all foreign concerns to the British officials while the British officials left all internal concerns to them. That was the way Seyyid Ali saw it. That was the way that Kirk's successor, Colonel Euan Smith saw it too. Although there might be 'friendly influence', such as persuading Seyyid Ali to sign a decree mildly limiting slavery, there was no intention of interfering with the sultan's authority.

This placid arrangement ended abruptly when Colonel Euan Smith was succeeded by Sir Gerald Portal in 1891. Portal was appalled at what he saw. Two months after his arrival, he revised the whole system by taking complete control of the sultan's finances and administration and appointing Europeans to the chief posts. For his personal use the sultan still had the revenue from his estates, and 250,000 rupees from public finance, but no more. As a result the harbour was improved, the streets were cleaned and the budget balanced.

The sultan and his court were furious, but to no avail. Even when Portal set off for Uganda it made no difference. His successor, Rodd, was equally determined, and when Seyyid Ali died Rodd exercised his power to choose the next sultan by installing Seyyid Hamed, on condition that he accepted British advice on practically everything. Understandably the new sultan began to become discontented with his restricted powers, and he shared with his Arab court a fear of the clear purpose of the British eventually to abolish slavery.

The coastal transfer. The transfer of the interior from the Company to the British government in 1895 brought the sultan's discontent to a head. He had hoped that he would be officially recognised as the ruler, but he was not. Instead, he was obliged to pay the £200,000 which the Germans had paid him for their coastal region to the British Company to cover most of their £250,000 compensation. The British consul-general,

Hardinge, and the chief minister, General Mathews, both objected to this as unfair, but feeling in Britain was running high against the continuance of slavery in Zanzibar and the sultan was forced to pay. As a gesture of defiance, he built up his personal bodyguard to 1,000 men. Fighting broke out at the end of 1895, but the sultan refused to disband his men until the consul threatened him by calling in the navy.

As it happened the navy, on this occasion, did not have to open fire. The next year they did. Seyyid Hamed died in August 1896, and Barghash's son, Khalid, attempted to make himself sultan by occupying the palace. This defiance of the consul, and the strong British feeling against Zanzibar, led to a major reprisal, when the navy bombarded the palace, killing about 500 of Khalid's supporters. Khalid fled, and Seyyid Hamoud, who was dependent on the British, was installed.

The abolition of slavery, 1897 and 1911. The fierce lesson of the bombardment and the compliance of the new Sultan Hamoud provided an opportunity for the abolitionists in Britain to push their case to end slavery in Zanzibar. The British government and the British officials in Zanzibar were afraid of the consequences, particularly to the clove industry, if abolition was hurried through, but the Anti-Slavery Society in England grew impatient at the delay. 'Why colonise', they said, 'if slavery was still tolerated?'

In view of this pressure a scheme was worked out which became law with the sultan's agreement in 1897. This made it possible for a slave to claim his freedom and for the owner (not the slave) to get compensation, but it was carefully calculated to prevent a rush of slaves from the plantations on one hand, or a complete disregard of the decree by the Arabs on the other. It was up to the slave to claim his freedom, and he had to do so through a district court presided over by Arab *walis*; if freed, he would be liable to taxation and would have to prove that he had a home and a means of supporting himself. Very few slaves could read the decree, and not many were anxious to leave their security, but by 1900 about 8,000 had claimed their liberty; a figure which abolitionists thought unsatisfactory.

On the other hand the 1897 decree did have a real and immediate effect in improving the attitude of owners to their slaves, because they could no longer treat them cruelly, or they would leave; and many plantation owners followed the sultan's example of allowing his slaves to become tenants whose labour was about equally divided between their own holdings and his own. When, at the end of 1911, slavery virtually ended, as compensation could no longer be claimed, the question had ceased to be important.

Surprisingly the abolition of slavery did not wreck the economy of Zanzibar, because clove-production actually rose after 1897, but to some extent it did erode Arab prestige still further; and they contemplated the future with little enthusiasm, while their debts increased.

Changes in Zanzibar, 1900–18. Despite the strict control of Zanzibar's affairs which Portal had instigated in 1891, the general idea of indirect rule was still accepted as official policy. Moreover, the Arabs were still very clearly regarded by the British as the ruling, land-owning class – rather like the chiefs of Uganda – with the Indians as the merchants and the Africans as the servants, and at the outset there was no intention of upsetting this arrangement.

Nevertheless a new order of things developed with the new century as the old characters disappeared from the scene. General Lloyd Mathews, who had made Zanzibar his home and served from the time of Sultan Barghash, died in 1901, having spent his last ten years as first minister. Next year Sultan Hamoud died and was replaced by his seventeen-year-old son, Seyyid Ali, who had been at school in England. The main personality who shaped the policies of Zanzibar was Edward Clarke, who went there in 1905 to suggest methods of re-organisation and in 1909 was himself appointed consul-general. His main idea was to make the consul-general's position similar to that of a colonial governor, with local officials responsible to him and with the ability to veto decisions.

Certainly the efficiency of the administration improved. Not only did Zanzibar city become the cleanest in East Africa but roads and telegraph communications were developed, and an education department began in 1907, although schools were not at first popular and by 1913 there were only 348 pupils in them.

Underlying these improvements, however, was a decreasing sympathy between the Arab aristocracy and the British consul-general, who put less trust in them. In 1908 British judges were moved into the sultan's courts, the number of British officials in 1912 was thirty-four compared with four in 1891, and the steady increase in plantations taken over by Swahilis was watched without regret. By 1911 Seyyid Ali had had enough of his artificial position and he abdicated. In his place came Sultan Khalifa, who reigned until 1960.

Zanzibar under colonial rule. In 1913 Clarke died, and the British government took the opportunity, which they had already taken in their other East African territories, of transferring the administration of Zanzibar from the foreign office to the colonial office. This helped in bringing Zanzibar into the general East African pattern. The consul-general's position, and that of first minister, were abolished, and instead the position of British Resident was created. He was to be supervised by the governor of the East Africa protectorate. The sultan was alarmed at this subordination to the mainland, and to grant him a more realistic share in governing Zanzibar a protectorate council was set up, over which the sultan would preside, and which included the heads of the main departments.

The First World War and Zanzibar's economy. Within a few days of the declaration of war between Germany and Britain the German cruiser *Konisberg* successfully attacked the British ship *Pegasus* in Zanzibar harbour. And that was all the fighting that Zanzibar saw. In general the war years saw a big rise in the value of her exports. The chief of these was cloves, which rose from £413,000 in 1913 to £759,000 in 1919. As the main revenue came from the twenty-five per cent duty on clove exports, this helped Zanzibar's economy and development in most ways. In the general boom the signs of the improved position of African peasantry were hardly noticed, and the decline of the Arab position seemed as though it might be patched up.

THE BRITISH EAST AFRICA PROTECTORATE (KENYA)

The way to Uganda. When the British East Africa protectorate was declared in 1895 no one set much value on it for its own sake. It was like a 'no-man's land' between the desirability of controlling Zanzibar and the Indian Ocean coast on one side and the desirability of controlling Uganda and the headwaters of the Nile on the other. As an area which linked the two, providing a route to the interior, it had value. That, it seemed, was its only importance.

So it is not surprising to find that it was casually lumped under the control of Zanzibar. The consul-general there, Sir Arthur Hardinge, became the British commissioner and his officials became the East Africa protectorate council. Some of the old employees of the Company were taken on to help organise what were hopefully called government departments. From the outset it was an uphill task, because the region had no existing administration, and if the British did not set much value on the protectorate it was certainly true that the peoples of the protectorate did not want the British. The soldier as well as the administrator was a necessity.

The chief concern at the outset was with the coast, where one of the Mazrui family claimed the sheikdom of Takaungu, north of Mombasa, in place of the British candidate. Most of the coastal towns supported the

Mazrui and successfully attacked Malindi and Freretown, so that troops had to be sent from India to assist British power along the coastal strip. It took nine months to quell the revolt but afterwards the protectorate authority on the coast was not challenged again, except in the north along the Juba river, where a rising took place in 1898 for the first but not the last time.

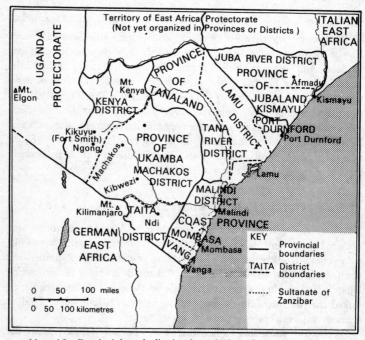

Map 15   Provincial and district boundaries of the East African protectorate in 1895.

Inland the protectorate, like the Company, aimed primarily at safeguarding the route to the interior, which traders had developed since the 1880s. Mackinnon's stretch of road from Mombasa had been completed to Lake Victoria in a rough-and-ready way by Captain Sclater in 1896, with supply points along the route. The main bases were in the Machakos district, where Ainsworth had established recognition of British power by four military expeditions between 1894 and 1897, and at Mumia's on the north-west corner of Lake Victoria, where Hobley, by means of military and diplomatic excursions, established a degree of authority over the Kavirondo region. Ndi (100 miles from Mombasa) and Fort Smith (in Kikuyu country, previously called Dagoretti) were also useful bases but they had only local influence.

The people from whom the British expected most trouble were the Maasai, who ranged over so much of the protectorate that their opposition could have been serious. Realising this British officials treated them with particular respect, and, partly because of British dealings over the Kedong massacre and partly because of the attitude of their laibon, the Maasai remained largely co-operative. Not so the Nandi. They came from a more compact region and because of this they were not thought to be so great a potential danger. In fact they were more aggressive than any other tribes, and several expeditions were made against them, particularly when they tried to stop the railway passing through their territory. It was ten years before opposition to British rule ended in Kisumu province.

The Uganda railway. The immediate object of the protectorate authority was to get the railway built to Uganda. Although a survey had already been made of the route it had not been easy for the British government to decide to construct a railway from Mombasa to Lake Victoria through land which was known to very few people, and from which no profit could be expected. Its opponents understandably described it as the 'lunatic line'. No engineer, for instance, had any detailed information about the escarpments flanking the Rift Valley, although these steep rises were serious obstacles in the way of the railway. There were also the long stretches without water, the tsetse-fly country, and the dense bush and rock through which a way had to be hacked. To these difficulties must be added the problem of labour, for the Africans in this area had no experience which would enable them to build a railway and had not even used a pick and spade. By now, however, the foreign office was determined that the line should run through to the lake. They knew that the Germans would construct a railway there if the British did not, and that communications must be improved if England was going to be responsible for Uganda: nor was the strategical importance of the country overlooked. Reluctantly parliament agreed to meet its cost, and coolie labour was imported from India.

The first line was laid in Mombasa in 1896, and soon an unexpected difficulty appeared: the danger from wild animals. The House of Lords was told of a party of man-eating lions which had halted the work for three weeks, during which time two of them had killed twenty-eight Indian coolies and scores of Africans. The two lions were killed by Colonel Patterson, who described his adventures in *The Man-Eaters of*

Tsavo. It is not surprising that many of the Africans believed these lions were possessed by the spirits of their dead chiefs, who had come back to warn them against the railway. Nor did the lions flee when the railway was completed; they would still occasionally stroll on to the platform and set the station-master a problem.

By 1899 the rails had reached a Maasai kraal by a stream which the Maasai called Enkare Nairobi, situated 250 miles inland. Here a transport depot had been built in 1896, and the railway engineers developed it into a major inland base, in preparation for tackling the Rift Valley and its escarpments, and here the capital of the protectorate was to grow. At the end of 1901 the rails at last reached Kisumu on the edge of the lake, at which point transport was continued by the steamship, which had been carried from the coast in sections by porters, two years previously (See Map 16).

The total cost was £9,500 per mile, which seemed overwhelming, but some of its effects were already clear. In 1899 it had saved the Kamba around Machakos from starvation by bringing in rice; it also silenced the last threat of the slave-trade (slavery having been abolished in the protectorate in 1897) by reducing the cost of carriage from 7s. 6d. to 2½d. per ton per mile.

The protectorate's expansion, 1902. The railway had been built to connect Uganda with the coast. Uganda was the strategic region and potentially the most productive one. Mombasa was the outlet. Sir Harry Johnson, who had been sent to Uganda in 1899 to recommend administrative developments, decided that as each protectorate was necessary to the other it would be best to join them into one. Sir Charles Eliot, the newly-appointed commissioner in the British East Africa protectorate, agreed with him. The foreign office thought differently. Instead of joining together the two regions they transferred the whole of the Eastern province of Uganda, stretching as far as Naivasha, from Uganda to British East Africa in 1902.

It was not just the size of the transfer which made it important, nor the fact that the whole railway line now lay in British East Africa. Even more important was the fact that the area looked like being good farming country with a climate which was attractive to European settlers.

The settler question. The distinctive feature of the first half century of development was the attempt to turn British East Africa into a 'white man's country'. This was partly due to the suitability of the climate and land, as we have just seen. It was also due to the decisions made by the early commissioners.

The railway was the factor which made it possible and which provided an excuse, if not a reason, for it. Somehow the railway had to pay its way, and this meant that goods had to be produced. There were no minerals, it seemed, so that the only likely alternative was agriculture. Did the greater hope lie with African or European farmers? In Uganda the decision was for the Africans; in Kenya it was for the Europeans. The man who was most responsible for making it was Sir Charles Eliot, who arrived in 1901 and left, after a row with the foreign office, in 1904. He was a scholarly man who thought the Africans were barbarous and in need of colonising by white administration and white example. Settlers had been arriving since 1896, but only in very small numbers; probably about a dozen were actually cultivating land near Kikuyu territory in 1902. Eliot wanted more. In 1903 a handful more came, including the man who was to become the leader of the white settlers – Lord Delamere. This wealthy red-headed English peer gave up his rich estate in England to risk his entire capital on developing a large estate in East Africa. Some people, like Sir Frederick Jackson, thought him a 'scally-wag'. On one occasion he drove a train off, leaving the governor and his friends stranded in the bush; on another occasion he locked a hotel manager up all night in his meat-safe for telling him it was time to leave. Other people admired his courage and determination, for he started by losing a lot of money through unexpected difficulties, and it was not until 1914 that his troubles were largely over and he had successfully established a wheat and stock farm in the Rift Valley. Whatever his defects and merits, it was Delamere, probably more than the rapid succession of commissioners and governors, who helped to give the East African protectorate its early character, and he remained the settlers' leader until his death in 1931.

His setbacks and achievements are of importance in themselves, and may also serve to exemplify the struggles of other white settlers. His first venture emphasised the price he would have to pay, for the concession of 100,000 acres which he obtained at Njoro cost him several thousand pounds in capital before he proved that sheep could not be run there successfully. This was land over which the Maasai had never grazed their flocks, and because it was totally unoccupied the government had been ready to rent it to Lord Delamere for £200 a year, provided that he spent £5,000 on developing it within the next five years. When four-fifths of his flock of imported ewes died, owing to a mineral deficiency in the soil, Delamere turned to cattle, but here again his imported stock was doomed, for the tick which carries East Coast fever abounded in his land and in those days no one dipped cattle to safeguard them from the disease.

Wheat. Equator Ranch, as Lord Delamere called his home, had proved a failure as a stock farm; it remained to be seen whether wheat could be grown there. First the land had to be ploughed, and there were no trained oxen or horses available. Next, fences had to be put up to keep out the wild animals. These tasks finished, Delamere looked forward to the first big crop of wheat on which he had staked so much money, but the wheat was riddled with rust. With this third failure Lord Delamere would have been ruined if he had not been able to raise a mortgage on his estate in England. Even so, his life for the next six years was a bleak one in a windowless, mud-floored shack. The money he was able to raise went on tracking down the remedy for rust. To do this he called in the help of a scientist, for whom he built a simple laboratory. Here research was done on the breeding of a rust-resistant variety of wheat. Three years later Lord Delamere harvested his first successful crop.

Summary of achievement by 1914. Now Delamere could give his mind to his stock, the remnants of which he had transferred to a farm, 'Soysambu', which he had bought near Gilgil. By 1914 he had proved that stock could be graded up in Kenya and the land improved. The years of struggle were over. That they had been hard can be read in Lord Delamere's own words. He summed up his experience at Equator Ranch as follows:

> I had 3,000 acres under cultivation—mostly wheat—on the Njoro farm alone.
> The result after a few years working was that sheep had proved a failure and big losses had been incurred; that the land had been proved unsuitable for improved cattle until the East Coast fever menace was dealt with; the wheat was proved to have come to stay. That the possibility of ploughing large acreages in a country where the plough had never been seen was proved to be an economic proposition; that large numbers of natives had been taught ploughing and working with other implements; and that I had managed to get rid of £40,000 in cash which I had invested in the country.

While Delamere was struggling to establish European-type farming in a climate with no winter to kill off the pests, others were experimenting with crops more suited to the soil and climate. Most successful, as we shall see, were the African cotton-growers in Uganda. So far as the British East African protectorate was concerned the products which were to provide Kenya with her staple exports were not of a European type.

Coffee was probably first planted by missionaries in Teita and Kibwezi in the early 1890s, but it was specially developed by the French Fathers of St Austin's mission near Nairobi, in 1896. For the next decade few people invested in it, except as a side-line, but then a rise in the world price of coffee created a new interest, and by 1920 Kenya's reputation for high-quality coffee was established, and it was the most important crop of the protectorate. *Sisal* had been introduced in the German protectorate in 1893, and in 1904 it was introduced in the Thika area. By the end of the First World War, it was next to coffee on the export list. *Tea*, although introduced in Limuru in 1904, did not make real progress until two planting companies came from India in 1925. *Rubber*, which had at first seemed promising, declined sharply after 1910.

The Convention of Associations. At a meeting in 1902 the settlers had formed a Colonists' Association which was superseded in 1903 by the Planters' and Farmers' Association led by Delamere. Later, other local associations developed, and in 1910 the Convention of Associations was formed and became generally known as 'the settlers' parliament' as its purpose was to put forward the settlers' views to the government. Their determination to make the protectorate a 'white man's country' and the influence of the considerable number of South African settlers, who had come in 1904, had a real effect in shaping the protectorate's development.

The Indian immigrants. Europeans were not the only people who wished to make the protectorate an area of settlement dominated by themselves. The Indians also had the same idea. Already Indian influence was strong on the coast, and traders had come inland in increasing numbers with the railway. They mainly came as traders from Gujerat and the area around Bombay, and not from the Punjab, as did the coolies who had built the railway, and then, in most cases, returned. The 'grand old man' of the Indians was A. M. Jeevanjee, who was a building contractor, a ship-owner, a general merchant and the originator of *The East African Standard*, first printed as *The African Standard* in Mombasa in 1901. Jeevanjee at one point had hopes that Kenya might become part of the Indian empire. But in fact the Indians' contribution to the territory's development was in the commercial sphere. They were the small traders who set up the shops. They were also the very large-scale traders. A recent historian has suggested that one of the Indian immigrants, Allidina Visram, was perhaps the most important person in the early economic development of East Africa as a whole. By the 1890s Visram was a well-established trader in Zanzibar, and ten years later he had over thirty branches throughout the territories on the mainland. His establishment not only sold goods but bought produce for export and acted as banks supplying loans to local government officials, as well as to individuals. Indians naturally felt that their economic contribution deserved recognition.

The rival hopes of European and Indian settlers led to tension between them especially over the questions of Indian immigration, the right to own land in the Highlands and political responsibility. It was the white settlers who gained the advantage. Eliot, on his own authority, gave instructions to the land office in 1903 that major land-grants should not be made to Indians between Machakos and the western side of the Rift Valley. Successive governors – Sir Donald Stewart (1904–5), Sir James Hayes Sadler (1905–9), Sir Percy Girouard (1909–12) and Sir Henry Belfield (1912–17) – found themselves caught in supporting the lines of white settlement which Eliot had promoted. Lord Elgin, the colonial secretary, in 1906 confirmed that certain areas would be reserved for European settlement, and although he made certain qualifications the white settlers accepted this as the 'Elgin Pledge'.

Land and labour. The whole question of settlement was beset with difficulties, because the protectorate was not an empty country. There were already viable African societies there, and some of Eliot's officials, like Ainsworth, reminded him that the first duty of the administration was to protect them. The same instruction was given to his successor by the foreign office.

To some extent it was observed. A 1901 order in council laid down that only crown land – land not already occupied by Africans – could be alienated to Europeans, while the areas occupied by Africans were to be kept by them as reserves. These areas were not easy to assess, in view of the shifting agriculture, but until after the war the area of land which the Kikuyu and other agricultural tribes could actually use was increased because of the access they had to areas previously reserved by the Maasai. The Maasai themselves came to an agreement with the government which was far from satisfactory (see chapter 9). Nevertheless, despite the troubles which were to come from the selling of apparently-unused areas to Europeans, the greatest early problem was not land but labour.

The African people could exist, and had long existed, by subsistence farming. They had no compelling reason to make them want to work while their numbers and standard of living were low. On the other hand, the settlers needed labour for their farms, and they put pressure on the government to let them use compulsion in obtaining it. This the government resisted, with varying determination and success, but in fact the problem was partly solved by the need to impose a tax to pay for the administration. A hut-tax of two rupees had been imposed in 1901, and later a poll-tax was levied. To obtain money to pay this tax it was necessary to work. Another partial solution was that a number of

Africans chose to settle on European estates and work there for an allocation of land.

To some extent it was humbug to say that the administration put the rights of the African population first. Once it was decided to encourage white settlement the white farmers, with their infinitely greater wealth and knowledge, were bound to be in the superior position. Yet the purpose was not wholly insincere. The administration did bring peace, the settlers did bring improved farming techniques and capital, the missionaries were developing western education and health facilities, and the all-round development did lift at least some of the African people out of poverty and introduce them to western ideas. Half a century after the war they were in charge of their country again.

Administration. The British administrators assumed too easily that all African tribes had chiefs and that the best method of administration was to work through them. In Kenya they gradually realised that this did not apply, and in order to create some machinery for local government the British district officer was expected to find a local person of sufficient authority to collect the taxes and provide labour for public works. Sometimes the unfortunate local 'chief' whom they selected had very little influence; sometimes he was not even local but happened to be an employee of the British who had proved useful. As a result the village headman's ordinance of 1902, which appointed headmen, was soon in need of revision, and the native authority ordinance of 1912 tried councils of tribal elders as alternative authorities. In both cases power still remained with certain individuals, and although the system did not always follow a traditional African pattern it did become reasonably efficient after the first decade.

The central government. Central government began with the appointment of a commissioner for East Africa under the control of the foreign office, as though the protectorate was a country with a ready-made government of its own. It was much more realistic when it was transferred to the colonial office in 1905. It was also more realistic to move the protectorate headquarters in 1907 from Mombasa to Nairobi, which was much nearer the areas of European settlement.

Government departments, and the number of their officials, grew rapidly, and administration through district officers and headmen reached out into one area after another. Where there was opposition military expeditions moved in to assert British authority, and there were expeditions, among others, against the Nandi, the Embu, and the Kipsigis; but by 1908 the African people had come to realise, at least partially, that their latest invaders were not passing travellers but rulers who had come to stay. They could do little but accept.

The political battle was therefore mainly between the government and the settlers in the early years. An executive council had been started in 1905, consisting of heads of departments, and in 1907 a legislative council was added, consisting of eight men, two of whom were not officials. One of the two was Delamere. But the council meetings were not of a policy-making type and were intended to give formal consent to laws, estimates and supplies. Delamere sent in his resignation. More effective in making their wishes known, from the settlers' point of view, was their Convention of Associations which has been mentioned already.

The First World War. By the time war broke out, in 1914, there were about 3,000 white settlers in Kenya, and for two years the administration had paid its way without a grant-in-aid. The war did not alter the protectorate's status, but as two-thirds of the settlers left their farms for the battlefield many farms were neglected.

Nevertheless the efforts had one major effect. The war council which was formed in 1915 to deal with problems concerned with the war in East Africa, included unofficial members, and unlike the legislative council it did have real power. As a result of their contribution to it the settlers were to win their claims to greater political power and elections for the legislative, when the war ended. Their influence seemed to be growing, but as we shall see, even more significant in the post-war years were the growing ambitions of the Africans themselves.

UGANDA

The declaration of a protectorate over Uganda in 1894 was followed by a troubled period described in chapter 9. The Kabaka Mwanga again rebelled, and was permanently replaced by his young son, Daudi Chwa; the Sudanese troops mutinied; there was further fighting over Bunyoro. The British government were alarmed at the succession of troubles and the expense which they involved, and in 1900 they sent their most experienced administrator, Sir Harry Johnston, to make proposals which would lead to peaceful and financially satisfactory development, with the emphasis on economy.

The protectorate was a very different proposition from that of British East Africa. Although there was much that was not known about the protectorate as a whole, in at least one area of it – Buganda – there was a kingdom with a definite king and an organised society. This provided Johnston with his starting-point.

The 1900 agreement. The three main questions he was called upon to deal with were concerned with land, taxation and government. The land question was the one which aroused the greatest controversy and which had the greatest effects. Before 1900 all land had been regarded as belonging to the kabaka, who had the power to turn a chief out of office, and out of his land, at a moment's notice. After some stormy sessions and compromises Johnston obtained agreement from the regents and the chiefs to the proposal that about half the kingdom's area should be regarded as crown land and that the other half should be divided among the Kabaka's family, the regents and the chiefs. As the division was to be in lots of square miles, this area became known as the *mailo* lands (after the English square mile). The number of chiefs who were to receive them was increased, after protest from the minor ones, until there were about 4,000 owners. This personal ownership not only provided an incentive to work, but also made those concerned, who were the most influential in the country, very anxious to preserve the authority by which they had been arranged. It is interesting to notice that after survey very little crown land was left.

The question of taxes to pay for the administration was settled by the imposition of a hut-tax which was supposed to be paid in rupees. This had interesting results. Very few people had any money, and for a short time cowrie shells and wild animals were acceptable instead (an elephant equalled 1,000 rupees), which turned Entebbe into something resembling a zoo. The effect of taxation in the Uganda protectorate as in British East Africa, was to encourage people to work, but in both protectorates the hut-tax led to overcrowding and was replaced by a poll-tax.

The constitutional arrangements developed the existing pattern. Already the kabaka was the accepted head of state with two katikiros (chief ministers) and the senior Muslim chief, and already he had meetings with his leading chiefs (the lukiko). By Johnston's agreement the kabaka's position was preserved by recognising Daudi Chwa and adding the title 'His Highness'. He was to be assisted by three chief ministers – the katikiro, treasurer and chief justice – and the lukiko, which was officially recognised as the Buganda legislature and court of appeal.

These arrangements succeeded in providing a stable base for development, and the leaders of Buganda were quite ready to accept that they were only one of the provinces of the protectorate in view of the fact that the total area which was recognised as theirs had approximately doubled since the arrival of the British. The province of Buganda was subdivided into countries, *gombololas* and villages, each with a chief.

Arrangements with the rest of the protectorate. From Buganda Johnston moved on to Toro, at the foot of the Ruwenzori Mountains. The mukama, Kasagama, was regarded as loyal, since he had not supported Mwanga or the Sudanese, and the paramountcy which he claimed over the surrounding principalities was recognised. Similar tax and land arrangements were made as with Buganda, but Toro was regarded as a completely independent kingdom within the protectorate, recognising only the authority of the British government. In 1906 the mukama's position had to be more clearly defined and Toro became a kingdom with the mukama as head, instead of a confederacy.

The agreement with Ankole was not made until 1901, because Johnston decided that the mugabe's power was not extensive enough in 1900, but a year later the surrounding chiefs were prepared to acknowledge his authority in order to achieve the recognition of Ankole's independence within the protectorate.

Bunyoro was regarded as hostile, and although Kabarega's son was installed as ruler no agreement was made for over thirty years.

The area of Uganda which was effectively under British control when Johnston left, consisted of those states lying between the lakes – Buganda, Toro, Ankole and Bunyoro. The effective increase of influence to the north-east owes much to the efforts of Kakunguru who was an extraordinarily able Baganda chief. With Apolo Kagwa firmly established as katikiro in Buganda, Kakunguru, who was a rival of Kagwa's, used his task of dealing with rebels to the north-east of Lake Kyoga in 1899 to develop something like a dominion there, with himself as ruler. Although, to his disappointment, he was replaced by a British official, he did illustrate how Baganda chiefs and the pattern of Buganda rule could be used in regions where no effective conquest had previously existed. From that time, the use of Baganda chiefs in administration outside Buganda became common. Between 1909 and 1918 posts were also established in the northern area and the West Nile, although development there was not comparable with the south.

Politics and boundaries in Uganda. The political arrangements of the protectorate appeared reasonably stable until the First World War. There were troubles in Ankole, Toro, and Bunyoro; military expeditions to assert authority in the north were frequent; nevertheless Johnston's arrangement of the country into provinces and districts, with a commissioner in overall charge with subordinate officials and chiefs, plus local councils, provided a working pattern; and in 1907 Uganda came under the colonial office instead of the foreign office, while the title of commissioner was changed to that of governor. In so far as it was convenient to do so the British worked through the chiefs, and the outstanding character was Apolo Kagwa, the chief minister of Buganda during the kabaka's minority. Literate, Christian, and landed, he typified the new aristocracy who were no longer dependent on the kabaka for their land. He also succeeded in combining allegiance to the British power which supported him, with a very real determination to preserve and develop his people's rights. The reforms in justice, administration and finance which took place during the war, and the maintenance of the lukiko's importance, were largely Kagwa's work.

Meanwhile the boundaries of the Uganda protectorate had shrunk. We have already seen that in 1902 the Eastern province passed to the East African protectorate, with profound results. In 1914 the Gondokoro and Nimule districts were ceded to the Anglo–Egyptian Sudan, but at the same time the West Nile district was acquired.

The economic development of Uganda. Sir Harry Johnston had found a country where ivory was the only export, and he assumed that the most likely method of increasing prosperity would be to encourage plantations of rubber, coffee, and cocoa under European management. For years afterwards influential men thought the same, and such plantations were attempted.

In fact, however, the main economic prosperity of Uganda did not develop from big plantations or from European settlement. It came from African-grown cotton. This was due partly to luck and partly to deliberate policy. It was luck that the portion of the protectorate handed over to Kenya was the most suitable for European settlement, but it was deliberate policy on the part of the administrators which made the alienation of land in Uganda less favourable to settlers than in Kenya. It was luck that a temporary world shortage of cotton occurred at the start of the century, creating a big demand for it, but it was deliberate policy by the administration which seized the opportunity by distributing free cotton-seed to African growers, testing the different types to find the best and eventually insisting that only the most suitable – American Upland – could be used. Cotton had been known in Uganda before the arrival of Europeans but it was not until the distribution of imported seeds by the government, in 1904, that it became a valuable export, and not until 1908, when the only type of seed permitted was the American one, that its quality was recognised. Between 1908 and the outbreak of war it leapt from providing 35 per cent of the total export to over 65 per cent of the total (£500,000). At the same time the 130 plantations provided only £23,000 worth of coffee and £3,000 worth of rubber.

The development of Uganda's economy was not only due to the

distribution of cotton-seed. It was also due to transport facilities. The railway reduced freight charges to one-tenth of their previous level, and made the carriage quicker. This made it possible to export cotton economically. It also made possible the importation of goods, especially textiles, bicycles, and books, and these tempted producers to improve their exports in order to buy them.

The railway, however, did not extend at first beyond Kisumu, from where steamers completed the trip to other ports on the lake. Few areas which lay far from the reach of cotton ginneries and transport could join in cotton-growing because it could not be ginned or exported. To enlarge the area of production a great effort was made to improve roads, with moderate success, and later, between 1912 and 1913, the Busoga railway was built linking Lake Kyoga to Jinja, which the lake steamers could reach, thus opening a large new cotton region.

The prosperity which came to Buganda and the Eastern province which benefited most from the transport and cotton, was encouraged and directed with the full co-operation of the chiefs, and as they prospered their families began to wear the textiles brought in; their homes became roofed with corrugated iron instead of grass, and the bicycle began to grow in popularity. So far as the British government was concerned they noted with satisfaction that in 1915 the grant-in-aid was no longer needed.

Social changes. After the old Eastern province had been ceded to Kenya there were probably $3\frac{1}{2}$ million Africans in Uganda, about 200 Europeans and 500 Asians. The Europeans were mainly administrators, missionaries or soldiers, and the Asians were mainly traders. To a great extent the economic and social development interacted. Sir Hesketh Bell, who was the commissioner, and later governor, from 1905 to 1909, was anxious that the protectorate should depend upon peasant production and not become a white man's country. The success of cotton, which he did so much to encourage, justified his policy. At the same time it made it difficult for such plantations as there were to get labour. Meanwhile the European planters were a sufficient force by 1910 to form their own association, and they remained a powerful force for another decade. So did the Asians, upon whose trade the community came to rely. Even the cotton economy itself relied upon the European and Indian communities, because it was they who ran the ginneries and arranged the transport without which the cotton itself would have been valueless. At the same time it remained a matter of argument whether the rewards were fairly distributed, because in 1918, of the £1,200,000 of cotton exported, half the money went to the African growers and half to the middlemen and exporters.

Missions and education. It is impossible to present a balanced picture of Uganda in this period without mentioning the influence of the Christian missionaries, which was probably greater here than in any other part of the continent. It was estimated in 1911 that in Buganda one in three of the population accepted Christianity and elsewhere in the protectorate one in eight. Both Roman Catholics and Protestants contributed, but the antagonism between them had subsided. In addition to the White Fathers the Catholics were joined by missionaries from the Mill Hill Fathers in 1895 and the Verona Fathers in 1911. On the Protestant side the C.M.S. missionaries held the field. Certainly in the Uganda Church, as in any other Church, there was much superficial religion, but there were impressive numbers of African evangelists who helped spread their faith, including Apolo Kivebulaya, who went sacrificially to act as the 'apostle to the Pygmies'. One interesting difference of policy between Catholics and Protestants was the decision of Bishop Tucker of the C.M.S. – who in his early days was appalled to see his congregation come to church with guns at the ready – that the Africans should take a full and equal part in running the Church. He ordained six Buganda deacons as early as 1893, and in 1905 all the pastoral responsibilities were in African hands and Africans were represented on equal terms with missionaries on the synod. The Roman Catholics, because they insisted on educating priests to the same standard as in Europe, had only ordained two by 1914.

The work of the missions had, from the outset, been closely connected with education. Before any Europeans came to Uganda it had been the practice for children to be instructed by their elders and chiefs in the traditions and ways of their people, but when the bush schools began in 1895, and, more significantly the secondary boarding-schools in 1902, the European style of education replaced the traditional, and emphasised the academic side besides dealing with agricultural and technical skills. Again it was the chiefs who were the first to take advantage.

Health. The early years of the Uganda protectorate were not without troubles. Apart from repeated famines in Bunyoro and Busoga, diseases were more deadly than any human enemy. Rinderpest periodically swept away over half the cattle in regions where it struck. With humans, smallpox, plague, meningitis, and influenza all took their toll by thousands, but easily the worst disease was the outbreak of sleeping-sickness which was first noticed at the mission hospital of Namirembe in 1901. Fortunately it did not spread over the whole country but was confined to certain areas of Buganda, Busoga and the islands of Lake Victoria. In these regions two out of every three people died of it. In 1903 the disease was traced to the trypanosome carried by the tsetse-fly, but this was only the beginning. From 1906 the drastic step was taken of evacuating all the affected areas and this, combined with medical attention, had a definite effect. By 1910 the worst of the epidemic was over, but in the meantime nearly a quarter of a million people had died.

Summary. The period we are considering ended with the war. Economically this was a setback, because shipping was dislocated, while plantations, farms and administration were either deserted or understaffed; yet despite all this the total exports did not fall.

Uganda was very firmly a black man's country, with Buganda as its most progressive province and with the chiefs leading their people into new methods of life, enthusiastically and yet with an independence of thought which made them nobody's servant. Nevertheless, in view of the massive difference in development between Buganda and the outlying regions, especially in the north, it is dangerous to generalise over the progress of the protectorate. The enterprising chief and his people, who could grow and market their cotton or coffee, had their way of life transformed; the cattle-grazers and subsistence farmers far from transport knew little change.

TANGANYIKA

The area of German East Africa, according to the 1886 and 1890 partition treaties, was roughly the same as Tanzania today, except that it did not include Zanzibar but it did include Ruanda and Burundi. Its history since 1886 may be divided into five main periods. The first lasted until 1907, when the government was chiefly occupied in experiments in administration and farming and in suppressing numerous rebellions; the second period lasted until 1914, and was characterised by a sincere, but only partially successful, attempt by the government to develop the country by paying particular attention to the African population and transport; the third period was that of the First World War; the last two periods are those of British administration and then independent development in conjunction with Zanzibar.

The German approach to colonisation. Although the British administrators were not particularly hopeful about their areas in the early days, the Germans were a good deal more optimistic. They expected their protectorate to be a financial success and a credit to Germany, so they set about organising research and seeking crops with more determination than their neighbours.

Yet at first they found themselves in many of the same difficulties as the British, and some which were worse. They, too, had very few men, and very slender financial resources, and unlike the British they had very little colonising experience. Like the British they found that although some areas had effective chiefs in most regions there was none, and the attempt to put in substitutes often led to oppression and hostility. German East Africa also had its settler, labour, and transport problems, and these they took longer to solve than the British. In agricultural research, education and map-making the German colonisers led.

The early years of German colonisation were sadly coloured by the frequent cruelty in which Carl Peters excelled; but in assessing German colonisation it is only fair to remember that it was the Germans themselves who condemned the early oppression and exiled Peters for his behaviour. In most cases the trouble arose from the local administrators using their authority and the laws in ways which had never been intended.

The German administration. The imperial administration was similar in many ways to the earlier Arab system. Only in three areas – Ruanda, Burundi and Bukoba – did the Germans consider that tribal authority was strong enough to be satisfactory. In these three areas they allowed the existing chiefs to retain their administrative authority under the supervision of a German Resident. These, however, were exceptions; elsewhere they considered that tribal institutions were too weak to be useful and a system of direct rule was set up. The whole country, apart from the three Residencies, was divided into nineteen civil and two military districts, each under a district administrator or *Bezirk-samtmann*. Each district was then divided into groups of villages, in charge of which were officials known as *akidas*, and in charge of each village was an official known as a *Jumbe*, who was often the local headman. The system was never satisfactory. There were only about seventy German officials, many of very poor quality, to administer the population of perhaps 7 million, so that the actual working of the administration depended chiefly on the akidas, who were usually Arab or Swahili. They were neither liked nor respected by the Africans whom they governed, and generally their only qualifications were that they could read and write and therefore obey orders. They had both executive and judicial powers, and were responsible for the collection of taxes, but they were not properly supervised, and an official German report later admitted that too often they were oppressive and dishonest. The general effect of the system was further to break down tribal institutions, and create a state of suspicion and enmity between the administration and the people.

The German land policy. Meanwhile, settlers were arriving, because the Germans, like the British, assumed that the best chance of prosperity lay in the encouragement of European plantations. By 1888 about thirty such plantations had been started and the number rose as colonists took up land in the north-east Highlands around Moshi and Arusha and on the coast at Tanga and Pangani. In view of this colonisation Germany declared its land policy in the land law of 1896, by which the whole of Tanganyika became crown land except for the areas already claimed by chiefs, native communities and individual landholders. It was also realised that most of the land was poor, and that its cultivators depended on a shifting cultivation; the *Land-Kommission*, which marked out the reserves, therefore reckoned to keep free for African cultivation four times the amount of land already cultivated. Unfortunately this apparently reasonable principle was not strictly observed. Unfortunately, also, time proved that the size of the reserves meant serious congestion, especially in the Meru and Kilimanjaro areas. This, combined with the constant demands for forced labour by the planters, and by the government for public works, seriously increased the discontent.

Early rebellions. It is not surprising, therefore, to find that the early history of Tanganyika was marked by a series of rebellions and punitive expeditions, the chief of which were the Arab rebellion, the war with the Hehe, and, worst of all, the Maji-Maji rebellion (1905–7) which is described in Chapter 9.

The reform of German colonial affairs. This rebellion was the end of the first phase of German colonisation. Missionaries had sent home to Germany reports of atrocities, and the Social Democrats had supported them in the Reichstag – the German parliament. In 1906 their exposures shattered the happy dreams of empire which the German people had treasured. They exposed corruption and cruelty in every colony and they gave the facts to show that all colonies ran at a heavy loss to the fatherland. The Maji-Maji rebellion, a rising in the Cameroons in 1904–5 and the Herero War in South-West Africa drove home their arguments. Reform now became the order of the day. A separate colonial office was created and Dr Dernburg was appointed as the first secretary for the colonies.

He appointed Governor Rechenberg to East Africa. Rechenberg, unlike the previous governors, was not a soldier. He had been a judge, and later Zanzibar consul in East Africa since 1893, and he fully shared Dernburg's views and believed that African interests should not be subordinated to those of the settlers. Learning from Uganda, he encouraged cotton-growing among the Africans; learning from British East Africa, he tightened the laws regarding the alienation of land and forced labour; and the settlers became convinced that he was determined to ruin them. Certainly he made no effort to compromise with, or please, them, and it was not until he was replaced by the more diplomatic Governor Schnee, in 1912, that the settlers ceased to oppose all that the official administration attempted.

Extension of the railway system. The second change in policy, which coincided with the reform period was the increased attention given to communications. By 1900 the only railway in German East Africa was a 25-mile stretch of the Usambara railway, which had been built in 1893 and was later extended. It was originally intended to run from Tanga to Lake Victoria, but the completion of the Uganda railway forestalled this plan. The next plan had been to build a trunk line from Dar es Salaam to Lake Tanganyika; this was actually started in 1905, but by 1907 had only reached as far as Morogoro. From that date railway construction went ahead at a much quicker pace. In the north the Usambara railway was extended to Moshi by 1911; this provided transport for the European plantations there and was also of strategic value by reason of its position near the boundary of British East Africa. More important still was the extension of the central line, which was pushed forward to Tabora by 1912 and to Kigoma, on Lake Tanganyika, by 1914, the previous arrival of the Lukuga railway, through the Belgian Congo, to Lake Tanganyika having acted as a strong incentive. Further plans were interrupted by war.

Economic development. The Germans made a more determined effort than the British to make their protectorate a profitable and creditable concern. They were faced with the usual problems – which crops would be most suitable; which method of encouraging them would be best? They assumed, as did the British East Africa protectorate, that white settlement would be beneficial, and by the outbreak of war the European population was over 5,000 mainly Germans, and was concentrated chiefly in the north-east Highlands. The settlers pressed their claims to land and labour as elsewhere, but the government administration did not discount the part which Africans could play, and after 1907 they put special emphasis upon it. The Germans also established a major agricultural institute in the Usambara Mountains at Amani in 1902 to experiment systematically with different conditions and crops including sisal and cotton. Amani soon became a tropical scientific research centre superior to anything in the British colonies.

Sisal. As it happened, the most successful crop proved to be sisal, which was introduced from Florida in 1902. It depended, as did cotton in Uganda, upon communications, and as the railway system expanded so did the sisal plantations beside it. Because of the capital needed for processing, the plantations were a European enterprise. There were fifty-four of them by 1910.

Coffee. We have seen in connection with Kenya that coffee was first introduced by missionaries in the Kilimanjaro area, from which region Africans spread its use. The Germans tried to develop it as a plantation crop in the Usambara area but it was mismanaged, and it was in the Kilimanjaro and Bukoba areas that the successful development of it took place, especially by the Chagga and Haya, who flourished as a result.

Cotton. Although some cotton had been grown at the coast before the Germans ever arrived, and although the government had encouraged its growth in the 1880s and '90s, the crop had little success until the market became favourable in the early twentieth century. The Germans encouraged African production – in 1902 and for some years afterwards, at the coast, they attempted to get headmen to enforce increased cotton-growing – and through their cotton corporation they distributed free seed and gave instruction in its use. Despite early fluctuations it became soundly established, and by 1918 a little more than half the area devoted to it was in African hands.

Nevertheless, at the outbreak of war German East Africa was not a profitable concern, for her exports totalled only £1¼ million, and subsidies from Germany were necessary.

Education. In many ways the German administration may be criticised, but in one respect the Germans fulfilled their obligations to the African population very fully. This was in education. The government, and more especially the missions, provided education for well over 100,000 Africans, which was more than in any other German colony and was an example to the British after the war.

The First World War, 1914–1918. The First World War affected Tanganyika more than any other part of Africa, for elsewhere in the continent fighting had ceased by the end of 1915, while in Tanganyika it lasted until the armistice. It was tragically unnecessary, for all areas in Africa might have remained neutral like the Belgian Congo. But this was not to be. The German commander, von Lettow-Vorbeck, wanted to keep as many British troops occupied as he could in East Africa, while the

British were afraid for the safety of their Uganda railway. In August British ships shelled Dar es Salaam and a German patrol attacked Taveta. A few days later the German government suggested that possessions in East Africa should be considered neutral. But it was too late; the fighting had begun.

In British East Africa there was an immediate rush of settlers to Nairobi anxious to volunteer for the forces. Farms were left, families were left, and a disorganised medley of units tried to sort themselves out in the camps formed on Nairobi race-course, in the grounds of Government House and at the other available spots. There was at first plenty of cause for worry, for the Germans had an overwhelming superiority of soldiers, arms and ammunition. But this superiority was of limited duration; for, as the British had complete naval supremacy, the Germans could receive no fresh supplies and were dependent on the land over which they fought. In fact there was no major attack by von Lettow-Vorbeck, and until 1916 most of the activity consisted of raids and patrols by both sides along the border. The British also made an attack on Tanga, but von Lettow-Vorbeck was given time to bring up reinforcements and the attack was repulsed. An interesting feature of the Tanga attack was the appearance of fierce swarms of bees, which stung both the British and German troops with painful impartiality. There was some naval excitement also in 1915 when the German cruiser *Koenigsberg*, which had been raiding British shipping, was driven up the Rufiji River – where her hulk still lies – and put out of action. But it was in 1916 that the main assault began on German East Africa. From British East Africa a force led by General Smuts, who had just finished a successful campaign against the Germans in South-west Africa, advanced across the frontier, defeated the Germans near Kilimanjaro and in March occupied Moshi. Meanwhile an army from the Belgian Congo advanced into Ruanda and by September had reached Tabora, while a Uganda force had crossed the Kagera River and in July occupied Mwanza. By the end of 1916 British and Belgian troops had occupied the northern part of German East Africa and established a provisional administration there, while von Lettow-Vorbeck and his forces were confined to the area south of the Central railway. General Northey, advancing from the south, drove them from the Northern Rhodesian frontier, and in November 1917 the little German army was driven over the Rovuma River into Portuguese territory. From there they were pressed northwards again by British troops from Nyasaland, but von Lettow-Vorbeck, harassed and without supplies, still had sufficient genius and determination to turn to the offensive, and actually advanced into Northern Rhodesia and captured Kasama in November 1918. At that point the armistice was declared.

CHAPTER 9

AFRICAN AND ARAB REACTION
TO THE EUROPEAN TAKE-OVER

During the pre-colonial period African society and institutions continued to change, and African reaction to the colonial impact was partly influenced by past contacts with Europeans. But the importance of the impact of colonial rule needs to be stressed, for it meant the loss of sovereignty. This in turn meant that the changes of the colonial period were not part of normal growth. The East African peoples, however, continued to exercise a measure of control over their own fate. The way in which they achieved this is illustrated here, but the background of events to the case-histories selected is given in Chapters 7 and 8, which describe the European take-over and the early colonial experiment.

The contrast between the Christian revolution in Buganda, which produced able Baganda agents to extend British rule elsewhere in Uganda, and the armed resistance shown by Bunyoro, is demonstrated in one of these case-histories. Reference is also made to the impact of Christianity, which was not limited to a message delivered by Europeans and received by passive Africans.

The examples selected fall into the period before the First World War. Between 1918 and 1945 Africans were acquiring the expertise and contacts with a wider world which enabled them to make the great leap forward described in Chapter 11.

East Africa in 1885, and European policy. Early chapters have shown that the nineteenth century in East Africa was a period of pregnant change, due largely to the growth of external contacts and pressures; high on the list of which were the Ngoni invasions, the development of trade and communications and the coming of European missionaries. Within East Africa there were also significant developments, the increasing strength, for example, of Buganda and the development of Zanzibar as a commercial centre. For reasons given in Chapter 6 Britain, Germany, France, Portugal and Belgium had developed a new interest in African affairs; as the British prime minister, Lord Salisbury, said, 'I do not exactly know the cause of this sudden revolution but there it is.' Pressed further, he might have admitted that English politicians had come to regard the Nile Valley and its approaches as a vital part of their Egyptian policy. Hence Uganda and the northern hinterlands of

Zanzibar could no longer be neglected; English humanitarians' concern with the slave-trade has already been mentioned.

European resources and problems. In the division of Africa, at the congress of Berlin, into spheres of influence, Britain and Germany took over the greater part of East Africa, and having done so hoped that administrative costs could be kept to a minimum and that their colonies would soon pay their way. In the early days this meant, in practice, delegating the functions of government to chartered trading companies, whose resources in money and men were limited. A contemporary writer declared that 'In all the territories administered by the Imperial British East African Company there are scarcely a dozen British officers', and the capital of just over a quarter of a million pounds available to the company meant that they had about 10 shillings to spend per square mile. Nor were resources much enlarged in 1896, by which year the British government had taken over the government of Kenya and the protectorates of Uganda and Zanzibar. As an ex-government official relates, there was then 'little more than an embryonic administration in the coastal belt, a few poorly garrisoned stations on the Uganda road, and an appreciation of the difficulties which had to be overcome'. High among these were the need to keep costs down, to establish a skeleton administration and to maintain a semblance of order in an imperfectly-mapped area inhabited by peoples whose languages and customs were unknown, a number of whom were armed with guns. In the late nineteenth century, the number of firearms increased so much that, according to one estimate, there were about a million scattered through East Africa. These, moreover, were no longer dangerous old flint-locks. They were Winchesters and Breech loaders smuggled up from South Africa through Zanzibar into the interior. The British consul-general at Zanzibar was powerless to restrict this trade or to stop the gunpowder, over 4 million lbs of it plus millions of caps and rounds of ammunition, which flooded East Africa.

In these circumstances the colonial administration had to feel its way, exerting its power when it had the resources to do so and making use of allies where it could find them.

Arab allies. There was a similar position in German East Africa. Faced in 1888 with the Arab rising led by Bushiri, which is described on page 98. Bismarck had to plead the need for the German government to vote the money for armed intervention in order to suppress slavery, otherwise he would have had 'to eat his words' that the trading companies would finance development without the help of the tax-payer. Placed in this position, Germany stressed economic development and, after Bushiri's rising, made effective use of the Arabs as her allies.

This policy was ruled out in Kenya by trouble on the coast, which broke out just before Hardinge, the first commissioner of the protectorate, took office. This concerned the succession to the sheikdom of Takaungu, north of Mombasa. In this struggle the British made it clear that they intended to be masters of the coast themselves. They showed this by using a regiment from India to support the more compliant candidate, Rashib bin Salim, against Mbarak bin Rashid, who was the legal heir according to Islamic law.

In Zanzibar, however, Britain's policy was different. It was not until 1914 that Britain gave up the pretence that the sultan was to be treated constitutionally as an ally by British officials. Long after that Arabs were still given the top positions in the country, consulted on government policy and, above all, provided with educational opportunities which were denied the African population as a whole. This checked any advance of Africans to senior posts, and accounted in part for their reaction in the first genuine elections of 1961, when they voted heavily for continuing association with Britain until they were in a stronger position, economically and educationally, *vis-à-vis* the Arabs.

The Maasai attitude. During the nineteenth century the Maasai not only terrified many of their neighbours and the coastal peoples, they were also engaged in a series of civil wars. These were mainly between the Purko, or pastoral Maasai, and the Kwavi, who were largely agriculturists. The wars had their roots in cattle-raids, and ended in the complete defeat of the Kwavi.

In these wars the Purko Maasai had been led by Mbatian, who was succeeded by his son, another Mbatian, about 1866. On his death, however, there was a disputed succession in which the British supported Lenana. Lenana eventually became the accepted leader of his section of the Maasai. This naturally helped establish good relations between the British and the Maasai and meant that the British had a potential ally where one was badly needed. For, surveying the inland scene, the British could not but be aware of the warlike strength of the Maasai who ranged the land on either side of the Uganda railway which they were building. The importance of this railway has already been detailed in the previous chapter, where it was pointed out that it provided an excuse, if not a reason, for the attempt to turn British East Africa into a 'white man's country'. This meant that settlers took up land along the railway line. Conscious of their own strength the Maasai regarded the newcomers without undue concern and were prepared to let them carry on in their ill-informed ways. It was only after Delamere, one of the earlier settlers, had lost four-fifths of his flock of imported ewes, owing to a mineral deficiency in the soil, that he learnt why the Maasai never grazed their flocks at Njoro. The price they exacted for an understanding with the British was that the latter should leave them alone and make no attempt to alter their way of life, and indeed no punitive expedition was ever sent against them. In return for this the assistance of their warriors was sometimes available, to extend the area of British control into the Highlands. Things very nearly came to a head, however, in 1904, when the danger of clashes between the Maasai warriors and white settlers led to the suggestion that the Maasai be moved into two reserves linked by a corridor half a mile wide. The northern reserve was Laikipia, and consisted of some 4,500 square miles, and the southern, which was of about 4,350 miles, ran down to the border of German East Africa. The area provided was, therefore, generous, but the Maasai were given no alternative, and there is evidence that the tribe were unwilling to abandon their claims to the grazing-grounds in the Rift Valley.

Lenana and the Maasai move. The arrangement covering this move into two reserves was made in 1904. In a few years it was seen to be working badly: the presence of tick-borne disease in the corridor resulted, for example, in the tribe being split into two. Lenana, the great laibon of the Maasai, suggested, therefore, that the tribe should be reunited in one reserve. If the Maasai moved from the northern reserve it would mean that Laikipia would be freed for European settlement. Hence the Maasai were offered an increase in the reserve in the south of 15,177 square miles, or approximately 1½ square miles of land for each household, which averaged five people. There were complications, however, in carrying out the move, and during this time Lenana sent the following message from his death-bed: 'Tell my people to obey the government as they have done during my life. Tell the Laikipia Maasai to move with their cattle to the Loieta plains.' This message had considerable influence, and the northern Maasai expressed their wish to move south. In 1911 a new agreement was drawn up and orders were given a year later for the move to be completed, but when the time came some of the northern Maasai changed their minds and asked for the move to be cancelled. Eventually, after considerable further agitation, it was completed in 1913. The manner in which the move was carried out has been strongly criticised. Sir Frederick Jackson, for instance, after saying that he was at first against the move wrote, in *Early Days in East Africa*, 'I then, in the interests of the Maasai themselves, changed my view, and was in favour of the move. I am, however, thankful that I had nothing whatsoever to do with the negotiations that led to it, nor with the move itself.'

The Maasai were not the only people for whom reserves were suggested. There was even a recommendation from the Land Committee that a European reserve should be made. This was not done, but after 1904 native reserves were set aside.

The Nandi resist. Another pastoral people, the Nandi, decided on protracted resistance rather than co-operation. Spared from the famine, locusts, rinderpest and smallpox which had afflicted their neighbours in the east, the Nandi had developed an organisation, which was adopted by the Kipsigis, under which they were led by Orkoiyot prophets. This gave them the drive to become the most dangerous raiders on the western side of the Rift Valley. A series of raids on the Uganda railway, which was being laid in the Nyando Valley, caused small military expeditions to be sent against them in 1901, 1905 (on this occasion the Kipsigis also were involved) and 1906. Similar expeditions were sent against the Embu, the Gusii and Kabras, but by the end of the first decade of the twentieth century resistance was, for the time being, at an end in Kenya. The fragmented organisation of the country ruled this out on a large scale, and the increasing number of Europeans, particularly missionaries, pointed to the advantages of acquiring European education and the techniques of the European way of life. The government, however, had to face mounting trouble from the Indians and the politically articulate European settlers, who saw to it that the policy followed was not a blueprint imported from England but one mainly evolved by local officials to meet the current problems.

Response in Buganda. In Buganda Mwanga, who became kabaka in 1884, was at the head of one of the most advanced and prosperous countries in tropical Africa, served by a group of literate well-informed men who were able to assess realistically the challenge presented by the Europeans. The impact of Christianity had also gone deep; the sincerity of some of the traditional leaders is indicated by an incident from the youth of Apolo Kagwa. One day he and a companion were sent for by the Kabaka Mwanga, who saw the threat from the Christian converts to his privileged position. The other youth was gashed with a spear and then murdered. 'Then the king turned to Apolo: "Are you a reader?" [of the Bible] he cried trembling with passion. "*Nsoma mukamawange* (I read my Lord)", was the brave reply. "Then I'll teach you to read," shouted the angry king, and gashed him too with the spear, and then took the wooden handle and broke it over his back.'

In 1894 when the British government accepted the need to establish a protectorate in Uganda they confined their rule at first to Buganda, which gave them a base in the Upper Nile Valley from which they could keep an eye on French and German advances from the west.

The Baganda now had to decide whether to co-operate with the Europeans or resist. This was never a matter of formal debate; it was a case rather of the Baganda weighing up the pros and cons, and seeing which policy suited them best. This proved to be co-operation. The stormy years described on page 100 had ended in a balance of power between the Roman Catholics, Protestants and Muslims, while the majority of the important chieftainships were held by Protestants, Roman Catholics played the leading role in South-west Buganda and the Muslims retained one country chieftainship. Key positions were alloted equally carefully; Apolo Kagwa, a Protestant, was senior katikiro, Stanislas Mugwanya, a Roman Catholic, had the other katikiroship, Prince Mbogo, a Muslim held an ill-defined but honoured position, the Kabaka Mwanga remained kabaka and the traditional framework of Buganda organisation was preserved, although the holders of power knew that they were dependent on the British. Co-operation between the two races was made easier by Buganda's advanced political organisation and relative wealth, which have already been described, and above all by the presence of the missionaries. Both races profited by the arrangement. But the balance of advantage lay possibly with the Baganda, who retained their administration in a modernised form; as such it was so successful that it was exported to other areas of Uganda. They also saw their principal rival weakened while they themselves were gaining substantial accessions of valuable territory. At the same time the katikiro, Apolo Kagwa, was successful in maintaining the right of the Baganda to a separate identity. In 1910, for instance, the Baganda instructed an English solicitor to support the lukiko's rights under the Uganda Agreement to allocate mailo land (land with absolute ownership, originally from the English word 'mile').

The British gained invaluable support from the able literate Baganda chiefs, many of whom were Christians sharing similar ideals; the Buganda government reports can hardly speak highly enough of them.

Attack by the kabaka and mutiny by the Sudanese. But an incipient rebellion and mutiny in 1897 showed that it was not only the chiefs to whom the few British could look for help. Threatened with denunciation by his katikiros and humiliated by the British for breaking the laws about ivory, Mwanga gathered a few sympathetic chiefs together and fled to Buddu, which rose in revolt and was supported by Ankole. The bulk of the Baganda, however, fought by the side of the British against Mwanga and accepted his infant son, Daudi Chwa, as kabaka in his place. Mwanga's rebellion also led to the inclusion of Ankole in the British net, for it had become intolerable to leave it any longer as a bolthole for those in opposition to the new regime. While Mwanga was still a threat in Buddu the second crisis occurred. This was a revolt by the Sudanese troops, whose inadequate pay was months in arrears. Despite this they had been used against Bunyoro and Nandi, then marched west again to Buddu to deal with Mwanga. The three mutineering regiments had then been ordered to march back east again. On this occasion if the Christian Baganda leaders had not supported the government by calling out thousands of their followers reinforcements might well have come too late to save the British, a point that Kagwa did not fail to note. From 1898 onwards he saw to it that Buganda claimed distinctive privileges. After these crises the country was exhausted, disorganised and full of troops. This led to difficulties between the military and civil authorities, and the home government decided to send out a special commission to reorganise the administration, which resulted in the Uganda Agreement of 1900, described on pages 118–19. The good judgement shown by the religious parties was now seen to have paid; although a minority in the country, they dominated the political scene. The efficiency of the Baganda chiefs not only impressed the government, it also led to an extension of the system by Kagwa's rival, Kakunguru, who conquered 10,000 square miles from Lake Kyoga north-east to Mount Elgon and ran it by the Baganda system of administration until it was taken over by the British, Kakunguru himself becoming saza chief of Mbala. The use of Baganda chiefs, however, became unpopular with the people in outlying areas, and from 1911 was gradually discontinued.

Bunyoro. Unlike Buganda Bunyoro never really had a choice of response. Resistance was thrust on it, largely because of the relentless hostility and skilful diplomacy of Buganda. During the first half of the nineteenth century it had a succession of weak rulers, and lost Toro. Bunyoro's fortunes, however, began to revive with the accession of Mukama Kamurasi, who extended her trading connections to include the Sudan. On his death an even abler man, Kabarega, succeeded, and challenged Buganda with reorganised regiments, equipped with guns. This was the point at which Baker, as described in Chapter 6, tried to secure Bunyoro as an Egyptian protectorate and was driven out by Kabarega. This success against Baker was distorted in England as evidence that Kabarega was hostile to 'civilised' nations – an impression that the Baganda were delighted to endorse. The Egyptian expeditions had of course destroyed Kabarega's Nile trade and made it important to develop southwards commercially. Here Kasagama, the mukama of Toro, shielded Buganda's western frontier and blocked Kabarega's plans; the latter, therefore, hammered on the kingdom in a series of raids. These led to Kasagama being driven out of his capital in 1893, just when the British commissioner had been ordered to lead an expedition to Lake Albert to find out whether the French or Belgians had got to the Nile Valley from the west; it will be remembered that England's preoccupation with the waters of the Nile was one of the main reasons why she took any interest in Uganda at all. The route to be taken by the expedition clearly had to be through Bunyoro. The expedition drove its way through but reported no sign of a French or Belgian agent, and built a line of forts dividing East and West Bunyoro. There followed several years of intermittent warfare, for the Bunyoro saw their independence threatened. The British retaliated by declaring Toro independent, restoring Kasagama and making a secret agreement to hand over large portions of Bunyoro to Buganda as a reward for their help, given very willingly, in the war against Kabarega.

Wanga. The British had another supporter in Mumia, who had succeeded Shiundu as nabongo of Wanga, on the north-east boundary of Kenya and Uganda. For at least a decade after the arrival of Europeans in his kingdom Mumia was under the impression that he was their protector and could direct their activities. When he realised the real situation he decided that resistance would be futile, in view of the superiority of the Europeans in weapons, and might well result in his own capture and exile, a fate which he knew had befallen Kabarega and Mwanga. So, at the time of the Sudanese mutiny, Mumia saved the lives of the Europeans in the area. Later, when the Eastern Province of Uganda, in which Wanga lay, was transferred to Kenya in 1902 Mumia was very disturbed, for there was no place for a traditional African kingdom in Kenya, which was under the direct rule of the British. For a time it looked as if an adjustment could be made by the creation of Mumia as a Paramount chief, but Swahili Muslims took advantage of the ageing nabongo, and his executive functions were removed. Although Mumia was a far-seeing man, and a legendary character among many tribes of Kenya, he was defeated, as Osogo points out, 'by the odds he faced as a traditional monarch overtaken by a colonial age'.

The policy of resistance: Bushiri. Reference has already been made to the coastal revolt led by Bushiri and the Ziguan Bwana Heri against Carl Peters's German East African Company, which forced the Germans to replace the rule of the trading company by that of the government itself. Before this happened the company had been driven out of all but two coastal towns, Bagomoyo and Dar es Salaam, and it was not until Major Wissman was sent with reinforcements that control of the coast was regained. Even then chiefs like Isike of Unyanyembe and the Yao Machemba refused to give in, and wide-spread anti-European feeling remained. The situation did not improve, for the simple reason that the same officials with the same ideas remained, including Carl Peters, who became imperial high commissioner for the Kilimanjaro district. In 1892 he was condemned by a German judge for excessive cruelty to natives, but it was not until 1897 that he was officially dismissed from the German colonial service, for 'misuse of official power'. He died in 1918. It was not only senior officials who remained in office. With very little money, and never more than 3,000 troops, the government had to look for allies where they could, and found them in the Arab and Swahili local officials called akidas, who had been used since the 1880s in local administration.

There followed a revolt by the warlike Hehe tribe, and finally the Maji-Maji rebellion in which the people as a whole rose up against the alien rule. Meanwhile in the Kilimanjaro area the Chagga varied a policy of skilful management of Europeans with military resistance, culminating in the revolt led by Mangi Sina of Kibosho.

Sina shows the flag of revolt. The other chiefs on Kilimanjaro feared this formidable warrior, who was famous among them for his skill in warfare and trade, and were concerned to conceal his importance from Europeans, who might increase it still further by visiting him. In doing so they out-witted the Europeans, who were convinced that Rindi of Moshi was 'king of all Jagga'. Yet it was Sina who was the first to install other chiefs on a larger scale, an accepted sign of power among the Chagga.

The basis of his power was an impressive fortress, which was locally believed to be impregnable; inside it was a store and an arsenal for weapons. Here he stored ivory from Ukuma, some of which might be re-sold to other Africans and some exchanged for cloth and guns with Arabs seeking ivory and slaves. Spears from Mamba were also usually included, for Mangi Sina appreciated the value of this weapon and was very skilled in strategy. He divided his warriors into groups and sent each section separately into the country they were raiding. Their instructions were to set it on fire and cause chaos. When this happened three lines of warriors attacked; the first had long-bladed spears, the second guns and the third short-bladed spears for killing off the fallen. Outside Sina's fortress you could see large banana groves which made this part of Kilimanjaro like a waving garden. These groves were cultivated by Chagga, to whom Sina distributed food and meat on a generous scale.

The end came when Sina was told to accept orders from the sultan of Uru, an unimportant country which had long been controlled by him. Sina refused to swallow the insult, ran up the red flag of the sultan of Zanzibar and prepared for battle, confident that his fortress was impregnable. So it might have been against mere rifles, but the Germans dragged machine-guns up the mountain and, after a hard struggle, the fortress fell in 1891. Afterwards the Germans reckoned that their effective rule of Tanganyika began with this victory, and the Chagga, as will be seen on page 140, changed their tactics.

The Hehe revolt. The Ngoni invasions had been a major onslaught by outsiders on the people of southern Tanganyika. In fighting against these invasions Makwawa, chief of the Hehe, won a reputation as a warrior that enabled him to lead the Hehe against the Germans, when his efforts to remain at peace, but keep his self-respect, failed. In 1891 he successfully ambushed German troops, killing 270. In the next three years he followed this up by guerilla warfare. The Germans were sufficiently disturbed to send a large force to capture and destroy his capital at Kalenga, but the chief fought on and finally killed himself rather than fall into German hands. His resistance shook the authorities, who continued to pay more attention than they would otherwise have done to Hehe opinion. Among his people he was idolised, and his resistance remained a proud memory which held them together.

The people rise – the Maji-Maji rebellion. The Maji-Maji rebellion was a mass movement which began in the Rufiji Valley area and rapidly spread, till nearly all the tribes between North Nyasa and the Kilwa coast rose in 1905, in a last great attempt to drive out the Germans. It was the most widespread revolt East Africa has ever seen, and began with the murder of all Europeans in the area. Officials, missionaries, planters and traders were killed almost to a man, so complete was the surprise. The revenge was equally horrible, for the Germans, finding themselves unable to end the rebellion simply by force of arms, decided to destroy the villages and crops of the affected areas. By 1907 the entire south of German East Africa had been devastated, 120,000 Africans were dead, mainly from starvation, and the region was again at peace – the peace of complete exhaustion. The causes of the Maji-Maji rebellion are still a matter for discussion. To begin with, there was a number of generally-held grievances against the new imperial administration, which was similar in many ways to the earlier Arab system used by Carl Peters's Company. Only in three areas – Ruanda, Urundi and Bukoba – did the Germans consider that tribal authority was strong enough to be worth preserving. In these three they allowed the native chiefs to retain their administrative authority under the supervision of a German Resident. These, however, were exceptions; elsewhere they considered that tribal institutions were too weak to be worth preserving, and the system of direct rule was set up which is described above on pages 125–6. In this, the actual working of the administration depended chiefly on the akidas, who had both executive and judicial powers enabling them to collect, in a brutal manner, the unpopular new taxes imposed by the government. There was trouble also over forced labour, and it appears to have come to a head in the Rufiji area, where communal cotton-growing was ordered by the governor in 1902. By 1905 the Zaramo people, who lived there, had decided to fight rather than continue to endure a system which wrecked their family economy and provided them with nothing in return. The uprising was spontaneous and spread like a forest fire among peoples who appeared to share only the bonds of being Africans, workers and oppressed. Here and there, there were pockets of Africans who ignored the appeal to revolt. (It was carried by witch-doctors, who scattered water mixed with millet and maize over the warriors and assured them that this was proof against all bullets.)

Chagga diplomats. In the north, after Mangi Sina's defeat, the Chagga realised that the age-old political game of rivalry among the chiefs had to be played with a few new rules. Chiefs' raids were stopped, but there were other means of becoming wealthy, and the chiefs were very clever at assessing each new European official, far cleverer than the Europeans were at assessing the chiefs. Dundas, for instance, had an assistant called Merinyo whom the Chagga regarded as very important because he went everywhere. Dundas did not think he mattered much and did not realise that chiefs used scouts as household servants and knew all that was in the files. They were also quick to see that their children could advance through education and trade. They therefore took advantage of these opportunities without relaxing their common opposition to the British. This opposition proved helpful in creating a spirit of unity among them.

The balance-sheet. In 1914 the British and the German governments could congratulate themselves that they had achieved their aims; German East Africa and British East Africa were under control and paying their own way. To achieve this their local representatives had been forced at least once to rely on the military force and financial resources of the home governments. Humanitarian concern and far-reaching diplomatic considerations had seemed to justify England in providing this backing, but once slavery was at an end, and India and Egypt independent, the position was no longer tenable; and the Mau-Mau rebellion was to signal the end of Britain's brief rule in East Africa.

In the eighteenth and nineteenth centuries developments in technology had made England the workshop of the world. These technological developments convinced many people that Europeans were superior to other races. By the 1930s some, however, could see that the European race was not necessarily cleverer, but simply luckier in its environment. In Europe the environment was one which encouraged men to try to solve problems by experiment and to develop modern means of communication. These modern means of communication have had far-reaching effects on the economic strength, organisation and culture of Europe. Africans had been quick to take advantage of western educational opportunities, and to show that they could produce scholars able to hold their own in the universities of the world. With independence in sight the African past was scanned with new eyes, and it became increasingly clear that European policy in Africa had been shaped by Africans as well as Europeans; while the Europeans had filled the dam the Africans had often influenced the placing of the furrows. Moreover, while idealists in both races often sacrificed themselves for the land and its peoples, most men had been influenced by what they saw as in their best interest.

In Uganda these considerations had favoured Buganda and relatively weakened Bunyoro. In Tanganyika the Chagga, like the Baganda, had also proved themselves quick to adapt to the dawning twentieth century, and were adroit manipulators of the Europeans, 'utilising each officer serving a term of his career on Kilimanjaro as another element in their stratagems'. As Mrs Stahl points out, 'They employed a whole new range of political gambits centring on the Boma [government headquarters].' In Kenya Mumia was less fortunate, largely because the kingdom of Wanga did not fit into the pattern of organisation prevailing in the rest of the country. Nor did the Maasai or the Nandi eventually succeed in making the clock stand still. The future lay rather with those peoples who soaked up western knowledge and used it eventually to further the interests of Africans.

In Zanzibar European achievements under Sultan Barghash and his successors misled British officials, who could not forget the Heligoland treaty of 1890, into identifying themselves with an élitist Arab regime, and advance was seen in handing over increasing power to this tiny minority. This resulted in an African nationalism which saw little to hope for and much to fear – a situation which was almost bound to erupt in violence.

In Tanzania the Hehe recalled their revolt with pride; and a clause was inserted in the treaty of Versailles arranging for the return of the skull of Makwawa from the Berlin Museum to which it had been sent. When Sir Edward Twining's efforts to secure this were eventually successful it was greeted by a long article in the local press. But the significance of this revolt was outweighed by the Maji-Maji rebellion, which was confined to no tribe but drew its members for the most part from small local societies, which by themselves were in no position to choose the pattern of their response.

Western man is apt to overlook the concept of time held by the Greeks, in which everything comes round again. We get glimpses of this concept in the part played by African spiritual leaders in offering fellowship between the living and the dead. The significance of the Maji-Maji rebellion may in fact lie not only in the devastated lands and homes that it left but also in the memories of the Tanganyikans, for whom Julius Nyerere spoke in his speech to a United Nations committee in 1956:

> The people fought because they did not believe in the white man's right to govern and civilise the black. They rose in a great rebellion not through fear of a terrorist movement or a superstitious oath, but in response to a natural call, a call of the spirit, ringing in the hearts of all men, and of all times, educated and uneducated, to rebel against foreign domination. It is important to bear this in mind in order to understand the nature of a nationalist movement like mine. Its function is not to create the spirit of rebellion but to articulate it and show it a new technique.

CHAPTER 10

EAST AFRICA UNDER COLONIAL RULE 1919-1945

After the First World War Zanzibar, Uganda, the British East Africa Protectorate, which in 1920 to the delight of the settlers became known as Kenya Colony, and German East Africa, which was renamed Tanganyika, all came under British administration. Economic development was an important part of the history of all three during the years 1919-45 when the foundations of modern administration, education and health-services were laid, and transport facilities extended. In all three racial problems caused concern in varying degrees; friction was most marked in Kenya. The Second World War gave a great impetus to the growth of nationalism, and from 1945 onwards the emergence of modern East African nations is clearly seen; by the end of 1963 Kenya, Uganda, Zanzibar and Tanganyika were all independent.

The effects of the First World War. In 1919 men were not prepared for the hail of difficulties which descended on them with the coming of peace. These were particularly acute in Tanganyika, and at first economic problems dominated the government's thinking. No armistice can turn the wasteland into productive use or restore the sacrifice of lives which war demands. In 1918 Tanganyika looked as though it could never recover. The military campaign which had cost Britain £72 million had cost Tanganyika misery such as no other East African territory experienced. Most of the campaign did not take place on the green and pleasant highlands of the country but in its waterless and fly-infested scrubland, where the army sickened and the Africans of the porter corps died of malaria and dysentery by tens of thousands. Disease and famine followed the army across Tanganyika, reducing the population, reducing production, damaging the upkeep of the Central railway. And as the war ended the influenza epidemic of 1918-19 also claimed its tens of thousands. 'Chiefs', wrote Cameron later, 'were without people, and people without chiefs. Thirty thousand natives were said to have died of famine ... Amongst those remaining great numbers had pawned their children for food, husbands had left their wives, mothers had deserted their children, family life had very nearly ceased to exist.'

Conditions in Kenya were also bad. In 1914, when the total European population was about 3,000, 1,987 joined up leaving a bare minimum to carry on the government and run the farms. A vast army of African porters was also required to supply the troops in the field. Nearly 60,000 were recruited in Uganda and the great majority of the rest came from the East Africa Protectorate. Losses in both groups were heavy, and the end of the war saw a sadly impoverished country.

The veterinary services had been too busy keeping transport animals alive to be able to spare much time for producers' troubles; African stock had been shifted about according to military needs, and without due regard to quarantine restrictions. Disease had, therefore, spread, and in 1916 rinderpest reappeared. Nor was this all; weeds and grass had spread over the ploughed land and through the coffee plantations. For many men, years of hard work had been wiped out by four years' absence. There was hunger too, for in 1918 there had been a drought and a bad famine. Finally the administration of the country, the roads and the railway had all been seriously weakened by the war.

The situation was made worse by the 1920–1 slump in world trade, which brought with it a heavy fall in world prices for primary produce. The price of flax, for example, fell from £500 a ton to £100. In the same short period, cotton fell from £35 a cwt to £5, and in 1921 coffee only fetched a third of what it had been worth a year before. This fall in prices was a heavy blow to countries which depended for most of their revenue on the export of primary produce. In Tanganyika, however, it could hardly have made the situation much worse, and the immediate strain was eased by the fact that the country was not expected to pay its way for some time. Kenya was, however, badly hit by the slump in prices, which put a very great strain on a country that in 1914 had only just begun to develop on new lines; and by 1921 the economy was £412,000 in debt. In Uganda, however, the fall in cotton prices (cotton was the principal export) did not bring the suffering that resulted in Kenya, and the protectorate's revenue for 1921 still showed a surplus over expenditure. This was because most of Uganda's cotton producers were Africans, who did not rely on it as their main means of subsistence. A fall in price meant that they had less money to buy luxuries, but they did not run into debt. In Zanzibar the Arabs still kept their monopoly of cloves in the world market, and the island was the least affected of the four East African territories.

The 'mandates' system. By the Treaty of Versailles Germany renounced all her claims to overseas possessions, but they were not handed over to the victors in full sovereignty. Instead, it was decided that the territories previously owned by Germany should be classed as 'mandates', and that the country in charge of their administration should be responsible to the permanent mandates commission of the League of Nations, to whom annual reports were to be made of progress in each territory. In all mandated territories slavery was to be abolished entirely, and forced labour was forbidden except for public works, in which case adequate payment was to be made. The mandatory power was also obliged to 'promote to the utmost the material and moral well-being of its inhabitants'.

Britain was given the mandate to administer the former German East Africa, except for the areas of Ruanda and Urundi, which were given to Belgium.

A review. A reassessment was clearly called for, in which attention would have to be paid to the idea that colonial powers were responsible for the well-being of the African peoples under their administration. The idea of African self-government, however, was thought of as belonging to the very distant future. In that distant future Africans might have a share, not necessarily the main one, in their own government. The British settlers in Kenya, however, had a greater sense of urgency, and pressed for a right to play a more active part in the affairs of the protectorate. In this they were followed closely by the Asians. Meanwhile the African peoples, in particular the Kikuyu and the Luo, began forming pressure-groups, called associations, to voice their growing grievances over the occupation of land by Europeans, and the growing European demands for labour. The government, however, persisted in regarding African associations as unrepresentative. When they wanted to know public opinion they turned to the native councils which they claimed were representative. The Kikuyu chiefs for instance were genuinely trying to get the young men to associate themselves with them, but this was a one-sided effort. The young men were not interested; they wanted quicker changes than their Elders, whom they looked on as the tools of the Europeans. In Uganda the political situation, was less strained racially. Most of the Europeans there were civil servants and the others took little interest in politics. Nor was there much trade rivalry; and until the mid 1920s the Asians were not interested in obtaining land. Land and labour grievances, which were disturbing Africans in Kenya, did not apply in Uganda.

Very little of all this was known or understood by the British, who elected the parliament, which, in theory, controlled the actions of the colonial secretary, who appointed the colonial governors and their staff. They were governing peoples who, at the beginning of the period 1919–45, lacked the means of making their point of view known. The result was that more was left to the initiative of the colonial secretary than to other ministers; yet the range of the business with which he had to deal was immense. Apart from letters and despatches, in 1915 he sent 17,237 telegrams, an average of nearly 50 every day of the week. In these circumstances the control of the administrative structure of the colonies was largely left to the 'man on the spot' i.e. the governor. He, it has been said by Margery Perham, 'combined in his person the roles of social leader, Prime Minister, head of the Civil Service, and for this period, Speaker of the Legislative Council'.

From this point onwards it will be clearer if events down to 1945 are grouped under the separate East African countries.

KENYA

The soldier-settlement scheme. In 1919 a new governor, Sir Edward Northey, arrived to deal with these difficulties. During his period of office the railway finances were separated from those of the protectorate in the soldier-settlement scheme, which resulted in the second large flow of settlers to East Africa being introduced. To carry out this scheme $17\frac{1}{2}$ square miles were taken from the Nandi reserve, and this grievance was ignored until the Carter land commission's report in 1933.

By 1919 the European population of Kenya had increased by 300 per cent to some 9,000. The African population, for which there are no exact figures available, had been reduced by war, famine and the influenza epidemic which swept through East Africa as well as England. The demands on the labour supply by both private employers and the government were, therefore, difficult to satisfy, especially as the damage done by the war had to be repaired and the population fed. The problem was acute, and there was much bitter discussion in England and East Africa over the degree of pressure which might be justly put on Africans to persuade them to leave the reserves and work outside. Eventually a further amendment was made to the native authority ordinance, to the effect that the consent of the secretary of state must be obtained before any compulsory labour was called out.

No sooner had Kenya steered her way past these difficulties than she was involved in a currency crisis which caused much hardship and was eventually settled by the introduction of a new coin, the shilling.

The full significance of the problems described on the earlier pages of this chapter lay in the future. At this stage it is worth recalling the limited aims of the Kenyan government, which saw its task as maintaining order and providing a framework of administration, all at a minimum cost. A country of business-men was not unaware that to accumulate one must speculate, but they left the speculation to the handful of European settlers and Asian shopkeepers, who were pressing for growth. The African people were still following subsistence agriculture and had barely begun to infiltrate into the towns.

Dairy farming. In agricultural development the lead was kept by Lord Delamere, who developed a third branch of farming after the First World War. Before the war he had shown that stock and wheat could be profitable assets to Kenya. Now he concentrated on dairying and in addition to building up his own herds established a co-operative creamery in 1925. The next year saw the export of the first butter from Kenya, and in 1930 the Kenya Co-operative Creameries were formed. This was followed by the establishment of the Kenya Farmers Association.

Staple commodities. The early development of tea, coffee, sisal, rubber and wheat has already been described. At the close of the last century the first passion-fruit, tomatoes, Cape gooseberries and potatoes to be grown in the hinterland of East Africa were planted at Machakos by a missionary, Stuart Watt, in an effort to make the little mission station he had established there self-supporting. He also experimented with eucalyptus and wattle trees. Experience has shown that Ukambani is well fitted for fruit-growing, and from this tiny beginning it has developed to a point where a fruit- and vegetable-canning plant has been set up which exports all over the world.

Pyrethrum. Probably the most valuable crop to be introduced since the beginning of the century has been pyrethrum. The fact that it was not grown in the country until 1930, although today Kenya leads the world in first-class products of this plant, tempts one to make encouraging forecasts about the agricultural potentialities of East Africa. On the other hand, soil erosion throws a menacing shadow.

The soil. Erosion is a threat to other parts of Africa, where the earth is baked by the sun and trodden hard by the stock, who occupy a special place in the lives of Africans. The heavy rains then wash away the unprotected soil, making deep channels. When the rains have gone these can be seen as big dry ditches, a sign that the land is being destroyed by erosion. In East Africa this menace was made worse by the rapid growth of population, and the heavy planting of maize, which was encouraged by official recommendation. It was mistakenly considered a suitable crop which would also provide bulk for the railway to carry to Mombasa. By the 1950s the soil had recovered; but since 1960 there has nevertheless been a steady increase in the acreage under maize, which is a tempting crop for small farmers with large families and little capital.

Introduction of the franchise. In 1918 it was announced that two European unofficials would be placed on the executive council; but this did not satisfy the European settlers, who increased their pressure for the election of Europeans to the legislative council. They pointed to their loyal support during the war and to the fact that Kenya had been self-supporting since 1912, adding that as taxpayers they now had a right to representation. On these grounds Asians and Africans had an equal claim to a vote, but this claim was set aside by the settlers, who declared that they were already represented by official members on the council. In 1919 it was also announced that the long-awaited franchise would be granted to the Europeans, eleven of whom were to be elected to the legislative council. Eleven electoral areas were defined, and the first elections to be held in the country took place in 1920. In this year the name and status of the East African Protectorate was changed to that of Kenya Colony; thus the whole country, except for a 10-mile strip which became the Kenya Protectorate, was now formally annexed by Britain. From the settlers' angle this meant the non-British Europeans could become citizens and so secure a vote, but it also had financial advantages, which were probably a deciding issue.

The Indian community: Devonshire Declaration of 1923. During these years, prolonged and bitter discussions between the British government and the European and Indian communities in Kenya took place. The end of the war had meant for India as well as Kenya an advance in self-government, and Indians everywhere were proudly aware of the aid their country had given during the war. An East African Indian national congress was formed to protect their interests and a deputation sent to England. The Indian government was particularly sensitive to events in East Africa, which it felt might further disturb the troubled relations that already existed between England and India. The Indian deputation was soon followed by one from the settlers putting the opposite point of view. After a stormy interlude the Devonshire White Paper of 1923 was issued, as a result of which Indian members were elected on a communal basis to the legislative council and the Nairobi town council. There was now officially a white majority of only two in the former. The White Paper contained also a very important statement:

> Primarily, Kenya is an African territory, and H.M. Government think it necessary definitely to record their considered opinion that the interests of the African native must be paramount, and that if and when those interests and the interests of the immigrant races should conflict, the former should prevail.

This was qualified by the further statement that:

> Obviously the interests of the other communities, European, Indian and Arab, must generally be safeguarded. Whatever the circumstances in which members of these communities have entered Kenya, there will be no drastic action or reversal of measures already introduced.

It is possible that it was only the Indian challenge that checked the Europeans from establishing a dominating position.

Early African nationalist movements. The First World War had widened the experience of thousands of Africans who had served in the army, the great majority being in the carrier corps; they had mingled with men of other tribes and seen how much Europeans varied. The need for resistance to be organised had also been noted. By 1920 the first African élite was beginning to emerge from the mission schools, and felt it was time to protect their own interests by forming political associations. At this stage these were aimed at the removal of specific grievances rather than an attack on the colonial system as a whole. In western Kenya these grievances were concerned with the continuous pressure exerted on the crown to control African labour, but the Young Kavirondo Association was soon persuaded by Archdeacon Owen to concentrate on welfare politics. In 1923 it was renamed the Kavirondo Taxpayers and Welfare Association. As the archdeacon saw no objection to members also voicing political aims a less 'left-wing' missionary, Dr Arthur, was put on the legislative and executive councils in 1924 to represent African interests.

In Kikuyuland the pressing grievances were concerned with land rather than labour, and the Kikuyu Association was formed in 1920 to defend African land, its members being mostly chiefs and headmen; but the next year Harry Thuku, a telephone operator, helped to found the Young Kikuyu Association. This was concerned with labour as well as land, in particular with the *kipande*. This had just been introduced as part of a new system of native registration by finger-prints on a card, called a *kipande*, which all adult African males had to carry. It was supposed to be a useful record of tax payments and employment, but it was misused by some employers, who commented adversely on their servants in a language they could not read. Thuku also attacked the doubling of the hut- and poll-tax. When his agitation spread to western Kenya and influenced the founding of the Young Kavirondo Association, and there was also talk of founding a militant East African Association, Thuku was arrested and deported to a remote part of Kenya. It was at this point that Archdeacon Owen stepped in and remodelled the Kavirondo Association.

Closer union. At the end of the First World War Britain was given a mandate over German East Africa under the League of Nations. The British government wondered whether the theory of paramountcy stated in the Devonshire White Paper could provide a common policy basis for the three countries Britain now controlled. This revived the old idea of an East

African federation. The settlers thought this idea was as undesirable as the local native councils which had been created in 1924. European worries increased when the governor, Sir Robert Coryndon, tried to press for an extension to Kenya of the existing planting of cotton by Africans; this had proved successful in Uganda. Nearly half the European farmers at the time relied on plantation crops, such as coffee, which Africans were not allowed to grow, but which absorbed a third of the total labour force of the colony. If Africans were allowed to plant cotton it would provide them with profitable alternative employment in the reserves, and the idea was therefore unpopular with settlers as it would further reduce the supply of labour available. The Ormsby-Gore Commission, which was sent out to report on the East African situation, confined itself therefore to recommending regular conferences of the governors of the three territories. Coryndon's successor as governor was Sir Edward Grigg. He found that the official majority on the legislative council was largely meaningless, because it was apt to disintegrate at critical points; Grigg was therefore prepared to support an unofficial majority made up of European elected members and nominees representing African interests. In exchange Lord Delamere and his followers would back federation. They realised that if their number could be increased – at this time it was about 9,000 – they would have a stronger case in demanding self-government. Closer union would mean that reference could be made to a larger number of whites, i.e. to all those who lived in the whole of East Africa. The Indians, however, would not have anything to do with federation, and they boycotted the legislative council as a protest. When the Hilton Young Commission, appointed in 1927 to report on federation, arrived, they found a situation similar to that before the issue of the Devonshire White Paper. The outcome was also similar; the doctrine of partnership was stressed, and it was made clear that England would not relinquish her control until the Africans could share in government. Finally a joint select committee was appointed to report on closer union, and considered that this lacked sufficient support; the members also made it clear that an unofficial majority of Europeans was to be ruled out. But at least an effort had been made to decide on a plan for East Africa.

Depression. In Kenya 1925 to 1929 were years of expansion and lavish expenditure, but in the 1930s depression again set in. The world prices for primary products were steadily falling, and Kenya was an agricultural country, and, as such, badly hit when the forward-on-rail value of maize fell from Shs. 11/10 a bag to Shs. 3/20 a bag, and coffee from Shs. 89/50 a hundredweight to Shs. 46/50. All over the world the mid-1930s were a time of falling prices, unemployment and general distress. In Kenya this was made worse by locusts and droughts, so it is not surprising that the budget could not be balanced. A new source of revenue had to be found, and in 1937 income-tax was introduced. This was a tax which fell particularly heavily on the European community – Africans in practice were exempt.

The Second World War. From 1937 onwards conditions improved; although over in Europe people were growing increasingly concerned about Hitler's plans for world domination, which led to the Second World War. Knowing the close understanding between Hitler and Mussolini, men assumed, when war with Germany came on 3 September 1939, that Italy would attempt to invade Kenya from her base in Ethiopia. Fortunately Italy did not declare war until June 1940, by which time East Africa was assured of support from South Africa. As in 1914, a high proportion of the population enlisted to help Britain; in addition the East African Railway's Nairobi workshop was the centre from which motor-ambulances, mortars, lorries, stretchers, etc., came to help in equipping the East Africa Command.

Conduct of the war. Once Italy entered the war, fighting began in the Northern Frontier district and British Somaliland. By the autumn of 1940 the position had improved to such an extent that it was possible to move from the defence of Kenya to the attack on Italian Somaliland. South African, Nigerian, Northern Rhodesian and Gold Coast brigades were now serving with the East African forces. After a successful attack on Italian Somaliland, these forces pushed on into Addis Ababa, supported by the Ethiopians under Haile Selassie. Here their progress, once they had begun to use the roads the Italians had built, was extraordinarily rapid, and with the fall of Ethiopia African arms secured their first complete success on land.

The entry of Japan into the war created a new situation. The importance of Mombasa was increased when East African troops took part in the capture of Madagascar from the Vichy French. In 1948 12,000 African troops were still stationed there.

East Africa's contribution. The nature of East Africa's contribution to the war effort then changed. Guards for prisoner-of-war camps and garrisons for the conquered lands had to be provided. Troops were sent also to help in the defence of Ceylon and India, and to other theatres of war. East Africa was also a training-base and a place of asylum for refugees from the Middle East and Poland. All this meant that greater emphasis had to be placed on agricultural production. In Uganda maize production increased from 49,000 tons to over 100,000 tons in 1943 and famine reserve crops, such as sweet potatoes, were planted on a large scale. The export of cotton, which was essential for the war effort, rose from £3,760,000 worth in 1940 to £7,026,000 worth in 1945. In Kenya African labour was conscripted to work on European coffee and tea plantations. According to the secretary of state this was done in order 'to enable the colony to play its part in meeting the food-supply requirements of the united nations, including those of the large number of refugees and prisoners in East Africa'.

UGANDA

Boundary alterations. In the twenty-five years since Johnston's commission the size of the Uganda protectorate was practically halved. The first portion to be lost was the eastern area; then, after the First World War, Gondokoro and Nimule districts were ceded to the Anglo–Egyptian Sudan and at the same time the present West Nile district was acquired by Uganda. In 1926 yet a third adjustment was made, by which the Rudolf Province, lying between the Turkana escarpment and Lake Rudolf, passed to Kenya. Although Uganda's size has been halved there remains a compact territory of 80,292 square miles, with a population density of approximately sixty-one per square mile.

Development of a cash economy. Taken as a whole, the land is one in which it is fairly easy to get a bare subsistence when things go well, but extremely difficult to obtain a surplus. (In a few fortunate areas, such as Buganda, the soil and rainfall provide a better living.) Development would therefore depend on the building-up of a cash economy and on the provision of market outlets. These in their turn depended on transport. By 1921 the export of cotton was accounting for eighty-five per cent of Uganda's exports, but the cotton-growing regions of Uganda were only linked to the rail-head at Kisuma by steamers across Lake Victoria. In 1912 the Busoga railway, joining Jinja and Kakindu, was completed and later extended to Namasagali. In 1927 it was joined to the main line from Kenya. However, it was not until the Nile bridge was built at Jinja in 1931 that the main line reached from Kampala to the coast. In the 1950s the Western Uganda extension carried the railway still further into the interior, and by 1955 it reached Nkonge, almost exactly 1,000 miles by rail from the coast. In 1956 the extension was completed to the rail-head near Kilembe, and between 1961 and 1964 the Rototo–Soroti line was extended to the Nile, and plans exist for building a new road through to the Congo.

Without the railway transport costs would have made profitable production impossible. For example, before the railway was built the cost of head porterage from Uganda to Mombasa might be as much as £300 per ton, whereas the rail-freight on cotton lint for that distance in 1963 was about £5 per ton. Delivery also was faster and more dependable.

With this development of the railway has gone a remarkable extension of road transport, to feed the rail-heads, and today Uganda's road system has made possible the production of cotton in all parts of the country where the climate is suitable. Between the wars a substantial proportion of public expenditure went on developing the road system. In 1920 it has been claimed that there were not more than 600 miles of road that were fit to carry motor traffic, but by 1952, 3,000 miles of all-weather road was maintained by the central government, and local authorities were receiving subsidies for a further 8,000 miles. While the use of lorries has resulted in a flexible transport system, the bicycle has made it possible for men to work further afield. It has also increased their well-being. The steamer services on the lakes also provide an essential link in Uganda's communications.

Once transport development had made it possible for Uganda to join the international economy, key decisions had to be taken on the direction in which the economy was to develop. It was decided that the stress was to be on agriculture in an African state. Labour might occasionally have to be drawn off for public works, but for the most part the indigenous people were to be encouraged to graft new methods on to traditional practices.

Cotton. Cotton-growing does not require large resources of capital; farmers can keep their families on the existing food crops while preparing the land and waiting for the harvest. Growing American Upland cotton, for which the government provided the seed, was therefore successfully started in the early nineteenth century among the Baganda. This was an impressive achievement, as at that time they lacked Western education and modern technological resources, and lived in a country with a poor network of communications. Their success drew attention to these handicaps, and, by providing a growing revenue, helped to overcome them. After 1915 the output of cotton had grown sufficiently to enable the protectorate to dispense with the assistance of a grant-in-aid. In the early 1950s the export of cotton brought in £15 to 30 million annually, making it easily the most valuable single export. The development of this crop was steadily fostered by the government, which carefully controlled the type of seed used. It was supplied free to African growers, and the industry throughout Uganda was generally supervised and assisted. The area now occupied by cotton is over a million acres. It is grown on plots which range from the size of a tablecloth to fields of several acres, where hired labour is necessary. The world importance of Uganda's cotton production lies in its quality rather than in its quantity, for its production is only one per cent of the world's total. Its price depends mainly on the cotton markets of Egypt, the Mississippi Delta, South Carolina, Peru and Brazil, whose staple is of similar length. Marketing policy is, therefore, important, and further details about this are given later in the chapter. Today the land provides over eighty per cent of the population with a cash income, as well as giving them security and a share in the economic development of the country. This, in its turn, has resulted in the need to recruit labour from the outside.

Besides expenditure on transport the establishment of the cotton industry involved capital to build ginneries (factories to separate the seed from the cotton lint) and to improve transport. The capital required was provided from British, Indian and Japanese sources, and until recently most of the cotton ginneries belonged to Indians, who occupied the position of middlemen. In 1932 India also bought almost ninety per cent of the cotton exports. Resentment gradually mounted, however, over the share of profits taken by the ginneries. The Buganda lukiko protested against the prices paid to the growers. Since 1952 there have been African ginneries.

Sugar and tea. By the early 1920s the government was experimenting with a variety of sugar plants with a view to developing this crop, which had been grown in a small way for some time. It is to a Hindu, Nanji Kalidas Mehta, however, that the credit for establishing the crop on a viable basis must be given. Having bought a 5,000-acre plantation in eastern Buganda in 1924 for growing sugar, he opened a refinery at Lugazi, which soon provided most of the sugar needed in Uganda and Kenya. Tea is another plantation crop which has a local market and has increased in value considerably since the Second World War.

Development commission report, 1920. While the development of sugar and tea arose from Indian and European initiative, Uganda's two main exports, cotton and coffee, depend on peasant agriculture. Credit for this is largely due to Mr Simpson, director of agriculture from 1915 to 1929. His determined opposition to a settler economy came under criticism in the development commission report of 1920. This pointed out the need for further development of communications. In doing so it stressed the advantage that would come from amending the Uganda Agreement of 1900, which made it very difficult to transfer land to non-Africans. But the report itself was set aside in 1922, and the acting governor declared 'Uganda's future lies in the cultivation of the soil and the growing of crops by the natives under scientific supervision by the Agricultural Department, and the purchasing and marketing of these crops by Europeans.'

Uganda's first development plan came out in 1936, and arranged for a total of £1,600,000 to be spent on public works. The next plan, drawn up in 1944, stressed education and health services, but after two years it was replaced by a plan giving priority to economic development. In this it reflected the views of Sir John Hall, the new governor, who thought the country needed to develop heavy industries to meet the threat of over-population. The appointment of Sir Andrew Cohen as governor in 1953 gave another twist to the direction in which Uganda was steered and illustrates .the influence which the governor had under the old colonial system. A census had removed the fear of over-population, and Sir Andrew believed social and economic development were linked together. He thought that if the standards of health and education were raised there was likely to be an increase in productivity.

Mining. One other factor besides agriculture must be mentioned in connection with Uganda's economy. This is mining. The mining possibilities of Uganda were not seriously considered until after the First World War, and minerals still do not provide a major part of Uganda's exports. However, copper deposits were found at Kilembe in 1927, and following the arrival of the rail-head there has been a considerable export of copper, which in 1962 was valued at over £3½ million. In 1961 a new and detailed survey for minerals was started.

The development of central and local government, 1921–45. The end of the First World War brought a major step forward in political development in Uganda just as it did in Kenya. In 1921 legislative and executive councils were established. When the first legislative council began no one seems to have realised the crucial part it was later to play. In any case it consisted of only six members – four officials and two European unofficials. The Indians were interested enough to agitate for two unofficials like the Europeans, and they eventually got these members in 1933; but their agitation was not as fierce as that in Kenya. The Baganda leaders also were sufficiently interested to inquire whether the new council would affect their position in the protectorate by the 1900 agreement. They were assured that it would not. Apart from this the new legislative council caused hardly any interest and had very little effect.

Educational development. On page 123 the introduction by missionaries of a western type of education was described. Missionaries were primarily concerned with the conversion of their pupils to Christianity, so the education of non-Christians did not receive much attention until after the First World War, when the Government began to take a more active interest in education. In 1925 a department of education was founded, although it only had £2,000 to spend. A vigorous policy of extending education was at once begun. Some fifty mission schools were given financial aid, and used as the basis for a new educational system. Another important step for the future was taken in 1921, when a technical school was established on Makerere hill to train artisans. This was later enlarged to include courses for medicine, surveying, engineering and teacher-training. In 1938 diploma courses in arts and science were introduced.

TANGANYIKA

Tanganyika, as the British area was renamed, was given a governor and an executive council in 1920. The governor appointed was Sir Horace Byatt. His task was to restore order and restore trade, and, despite the after-effects of war and the world slump of the early 1920s, he did both. When he left in 1925 Tanganyika was exporting twice as much as she had exported before the war, and from 1923 no longer needed British grants-in-aid. It was a remarkable achievement and provided a firm foundation on which Sir Donald Cameron could build. He was a man of a very different type. Byatt was almost excessively cautious; too much of an invalid to get to know the country through extensive tours, he was content to leave native administration alone and avoid an extension of European settlement.

The policy of Sir Donald Cameron. Sir Donald Cameron, who had been chief secretary in Nigeria, succeeded Byatt in 1925. He was the architect of modern Tanganyika, and the administrative policy which he adopted was the exact opposite to that of the Germans. They had ruled mainly through alien administrators, who had encouraged the disintegration of tribal authority. Cameron's policy was to revive that authority and allow it to rule. There were two main considerations on which he based his policy. The first was that he had too few European officials to set up an efficient administration dependent on them alone. The second was that the mandate itself implied that the aim of government should be to enable the people of Tanganyika to stand by themselves, however distant the time might be when they should be able to do so.

The reorganisation of administration: indirect rule. Cameron's administration has sometimes been described as indirect rule: he himself preferred to call it native administration. Tanganyika, as he organised it, was divided into eleven provinces, each under a provincial commissioner, whose area was divided into districts under district commissioners. In this there was nothing unusual, except Cameron's insistence on obtaining frank opinions from his subordinates, and co-ordination of policy, based on what he saw on extensive tours. These convinced him that the system of akidas must stop. In its place he deliberately revived African institutions. In each district he sought to discover not who claimed to rule but who in fact was accepted by the tribe – or group of tribes – as the rightful ruler. The only places where he failed to choose a satisfactory authority were in the coastal districts of the extreme south, where Ngoni invasions, the disruptions caused by the Arab slave-traders and the Maji-Maji rebellion had broken tribal life into smaller fragments than elsewhere. But throughout the rest of Tanganyika, except the Bukoba district, where the chief's authority had never been destroyed, Cameron chose his authorities so well that the system rapidly proved a success. Good chiefs found that they got their correct pay, inactive ones received nothing and the treasury saved thousands of pounds. Generally the native authority was made responsible for the maintenance of good order and government among the Africans in its area. To enable it to enforce its powers it was given a native court, with limited powers of punishment and imprisonment. In addition the native authorities were made responsible for the collection of taxes. It was to Cameron also, who always valued criticism highly, that the early introduction of a legislative council in 1926 was due.

Economic development. Tanganyika is about the same size as Nigeria, or, to take another comparison, it is roughly equal in area to France and Germany combined. From the economic point of view its size is its handicap, because the fertile areas are on its edges – on the coast, the lake, the highlands – whereas the centre is mainly arid bush, often inhabited by the tsetse fly. Moreover, enormous communication problems arise. Even in 1960 the fertile southern Highlands had no railway to link the area with markets and the town of Iringa was dependent on an infrequent bus service, passengers on which were advised to carry their own food supplies if they did not want to fast. In 1925 the first step was to ban head porterage. Next Cameron improved old roads and built new ones, which enabled the Africans to reach markets for their goods for the first time. When he left in 1931 the total mileage of roads was 3,587. This was clearly inadequate for a country four times the size of Great Britain, but further advances were checked by the financial crisis which hit Europe in that year. Britain could support the old argument that the colonies should maintain themselves with the practical point that there was no money available. Thirty years later, however, the total mileage had increased to 18,278 miles, in addition to 8,000 miles of dirt tracks. As Tanganyika was a mandated area and not a colony Cameron could only borrow money in London if parliament would guarantee the interest. He did, however, secure funds to extend the railway line from Tabora to Mwanza (the extension of the line to Mwanza opened up the valuable producing areas around Lake Victoria, and provided closer links with Kenya and Uganda through the lake steamers), and from Moshi to Arusha.

He also directed agricultural officers to show Africans how to grow new cash crops as well as improve the old ones. The result was that the national income of Tanganyika, which was a primary producing country, actually went up during the period 1925–30 when world prices for primary products were dropping.

Education. Cameron's main concern, though, was to raise the standard of education, for without education preparation for independence could not succeed.

The Germans had laid a foundation of government schools, which were supported by the Catholic and Protestant missions, and on the eve of the First World War the government was able to communicate with headmen by writing in Swahili. This indicates a higher level of literacy than was reached in Uganda or Kenya. Then came the war with its devastating effects, in which education was included. Mission schools in particular were affected, as many of the original staff were not allowed to return because they had been on the side of the Germans; and although their replacements were of the same denomination, their languages and background were different, so there was little at first on which they could build. The first step forward was, however, taken in 1920, when a department of education was founded, and two years later Tabora school was founded for the sons and heirs of chiefs. It was run on British public-school lines, adapted to an African environment. By 1935 the tribal organization of the school had gone; less stress was placed on vocational objectives, and more on higher education. Ten years earlier, in 1925, further encouragement had been given to education by the publication of a report on 'Education in Tropical African Territories'. This urged governments to build schools of their own, as well as assisting missionary societies, and resulted in government spending on education going up by 500 per cent in the next four years.

Until the end of the Second World War there were few other changes, and 'What Tabora does today other schools do tomorrow' was still widely quoted; but by the end of the 1940s the Roman Catholic school of Pugu, and the U.M.C.A. (Universities Mission to Central Africa) school of Minaki were flourishing and entering pupils for Cambridge school certificate. But the ground was still only scratched; by 1947 only thirteen-and-a-half per cent of children of primary-school age were being educated.

Local government. Cameron's policy of indirect rule increased the power of active chiefs, and gave African courts a recognized place in the administration. At the same time Africans were moving outside their tribal society and new customs were developing. Tanganyika, however, remained a rural society in outlook.

Dar es Salaam. A port occupies a key position in the economy of a country, and many of the changes that took place in the last hundred years in Tanganyika are mirrored in the history of Dar es Salaam.

According to the *History of Dar es Salaam* the first settlers on the site of the modern town were Arabs. In the course of time, a fishing village, called Mzizima, grew up here, near an inland creek some 25 miles from the old township of Bagamoyo. By the early nineteenth century caravans organised from Zanzibar were setting out for the interior from a point about 15 miles south-west of Mzizima. In 1862 Seyyid Majid's attention was directed to the village and its site on a safe harbour. He at once saw its possibilities as a base for trade with the interior, and even spoke of transferring his capital to what was beginning to be called Dar es Salaam, 'a haven of peace'. By 1866 he had a summer palace there, and building had begun by the side of the harbour. By that time he had only two more years to live, and Seyyid Barghash, who succeeded him, was not interested in the possibilities of Dar es Salaam. Interest in the place revived briefly when work began on the construction of a road to Lake Nyasa, but when this was abandoned interest in Dar es Salaam as a starting-point for caravans died too.

In 1885 the Society for German Colonisation secured its use for trading, and six years later the headquarters of German East Africa was transferred there from Bagamoyo. By the Anglo–German Agreement of 1886 England promised to support the company in securing the lease of the customs at Dar es Salaam, and in 1887 a German warship arrived there, carrying Hauptman Leue, the representative of the company, who proceeded to buy the town from the *Jumbe.* Eleven months later the Germans obtained a further concession over the coast between the Rurrima and the Umba. As Hemedi bin Abdullah bin Said al-Buhriy wrote:

> At Kilwa and Dar-Es-Salaam
> There was a plague of Europeans;
> There was no free speech
> They had throttled the country.
> To Tanga they came daily
> Asking for houses.

They certainly soon became very unpopular, largely through lack of consideration. In Tanga dogs belonging to Germans were allowed to get into the Friday mosque during Ramadan. Many Arabs also feared that the Germans would interfere with the ivory- slave- and rubber-trade. Protests were made to the sultan at Zanzibar but he felt powerless to interfere. The rising tide of indignation led to Bushiri's revolt which forced the German government to take over from the company. Two years later the government moved their headquarters from Bagamoyo to Dar es Salaam.

At that time the town had less than 500 inhabitants, but by 1896 these had increased to 13,000 of whom about 1,000 were Asians. During the First World War the town was captured by the British, in 1916, and used as the base for the conquest of the country. Today few of the old Arab and German houses remain, and multi-storey buildings signal its development as the capital of Tanzania. It is not only the main outlet for most of the country's produce, it is also a transit-port for the Democratic Republic of the Congo and the coastal terminus of the Central railway; since 1954 it has had an airport. Apart from being the centre of a key communications system, the town has developed a number of local industries; these include metal boxes, soap, paint and cigarette manufactures.

Second World War. Before Sir Donald Cameron left the territory economic difficulties had appeared. A big drop in world prices had disastrous results. In 1930, for example, sisal, which was the country's chief export crop, was selling for only £21 a ton; yet a year earlier it had fetched £30. Nor was this the end; the price soon fell further to £12 a ton. The year 1930 was also a bad one for coffee; although the crop was larger than in 1929 it was sold for thirty-three per cent less money. Fortunately subsistence crops were less affected; but the general development of the country was halted, plans for further development of communications were stopped and expenditure on education and medicine cut down. In order to raise revenue in these difficult times, a poll-tax was introduced. By this time the government was under growing pressure from the Germans, who were settling in increasing numbers in the country. Other Europeans, who feared that Germany might regain control of the country, supported the policy of closer union as a protection against this. By 1935, the Tanganyika economy was recovering. Four years later the Second World War broke out. This time, however, Tanganyika was not a battle-field. Its chief contribution in this war was in supplying new materials and manpower. For the first time the King's African Rifles went overseas, and Africans saw fighting in other continents, served in forces which ignored tribal barriers, and helped drive out a European power from Ethiopia and restore its African ruler. In 1942 Tanganyika troops went on to fight the Vichy French in Madagascar. A year later those serving in the King's African Rifles went to Ceylon en route for the Burma campaign. At home the German settlers were interned (they were so sure of ultimate victory that they put up little resistance), and Tanganyika drained her reserve funds to support the British war effort. The strain on food supplies was considerable, as Tanganyika made great efforts to remain self-supporting. The standard of clothing in country districts also inevitably fell, and bark-cloth and skins were usually worn. But throughout the war the morale of the population was high, despite the problems of food supplies, the deterioration of transport and the shortcomings in administration. By 1945 the need for post-war planning was generally recognised.

ZANZIBAR

Legislative council set up and the post of high commissioner abolished. Although it had been a wise step to transfer the administration of Zanzibar from the foreign office to the colonial office, which was better able to deal with its problems, a few years' experience showed that this was also not entirely satisfactory. For one thing, too much delay was caused by referring matters from Zanzibar to the high commissioner who, as governor of East Africa, was resident in Nairobi. In 1925, therefore, the post of high commissioner was abolished. At the same time, the protectorate council was also abolished, largely because it was out of touch with the unofficial community. In its place a legislative council was set up, with an official majority, but containing also unofficial members who were to be nominated after the advice of leading unofficial bodies had been secured.

Advances to self-government. Before this change could be introduced, the sultan's consent had to be obtained, because it meant that his power of legislating by issuing decrees would be limited. As the sultan was anxious that his subjects should have a greater share in the work of government he agreed. At the same time a small executive council was set up to advise him and to discuss what measures the government should introduce into the legislative council.

Local government. For purposes of local government Zanzibar was divided into three districts, Pemba Island, Urban Zanzibar and rural Zanzibar. Each district was in the charge of a district commissioner, under the general direction of the senior commissioner, and was subdivided into *mudirias*, and further subdivided into *shehias*.

Economic progress. In the reign of Seyyid Hamoud efforts were made by the new department of agriculture to find fresh crops suitable for a tropical climate. These efforts were successful in that it was shown that it would pay the people of Zanzibar to experiment with a far larger variety of crops, such as coffee, tea, cocoa, cinnamon and nutmegs. But the inhabitants were not convinced that the new crops would pay them better than their old favourites, cloves and coconuts, and it was realised that the best hope for the future lay in the education of the young. In 1907, therefore, it was decided to start a department of education, and primary schools were set up in Zanzibar town and some of the chief villages. Despite this the Zanzibaris continued to concentrate on their two main crops, reckoning to import foodstuffs. The Second World War shook their prejudices, and some saw the need for subsistence farming.

The development of education. Education in Zanzibar and Pemba began with the establishment of schools for the study of the Koran. These Koran schools, which were later scattered in their hundreds throughout the islands, still provided the early education of most of the inhabitants. Further developments came from Christian missions; in 1870 the U.M.C.A. started Bishop Tozer's school, for the children of freed slaves. Individuals also founded schools: among these were Seyyid Hamoud who allowed the government school for the sons of his relatives and other leading Arabs to meet in one of his palaces; and by 1890 leaders of the different Indian communities had collected money for a school which became known as the Sir Euan Smith Madressa. This later received financial support from the government. However, lack of public support, and the First World War, resulted in little progress being made until a Koran class was formed in every government school. Greater numbers then began to come forward for the primary education which the government provided free. However, it was not until 1935 that the government was able to start a secondary school for boys, which offered courses leading to school certificate.

CHAPTER 11

THE EMERGENCE OF MODERN
EAST AFRICAN NATIONS 1945–1963

The Second World War and nationalism. It has been pointed out earlier that in the Second World War Africans saw service overseas for the first time, with the result that, as Oginga Odinga wrote, 'Here were men who had overcome their fear of the power of the White Man; they were trained soldiers who had fought in his war, with his weapons, and who could put their fighting experience to use in the freedom struggle.' Shooting-lessons, he adds, were given 'under cover of dynamiting at stone quarries'. Experience had also developed confidence, and many sought new openings, in the retail trade for instance and as buyers of African produce. Others had acquired skills such as driving, with which they hoped to earn a better living after the war, often in vain – and this was a cause of frustration.

The seeds of nationalism had been sown, but the harvest was still in the future. One of the events during his period as governor which gave Cameron most satisfaction was the foundation of the Tanganyika African Association (T.A.A.) which provided Africans with a platform on which they could discuss problems and meet Europeans on equal terms. Among the foundation members were three professional men, Martin Kayamba, Mdachi Shariff and Kleist Sykes. After the Second World War two of the sons of Kleist Sykes were among the returning soldiers. Effective nationalism among the people was not, however, born until the meeting of the Tanganyika African Association at Dar es Salaam in 1954, when the aims and constitution of a new organization called the Tanganyika African National Union (T.A.N.U.) were drafted.

In Kenya the First World War had been followed by the grant of representative government; and the advance to self-government was further accelerated by the Second World War, in which Africans gained experience in a wider world. In 1944 the first African, Mr Eliud Mathu, a graduate of Balliol College, Oxford, took his seat in the legislative council. There were now two representatives of African interests. In 1948, when this number was increased to four, all of whom were Africans, there was for the first time an unofficial majority in the legislative council. In other words, the majority of the members of the council were there because they had been elected and not because of their position as officials. But these constitutional advances were no longer sufficient to satisfy either the ex-soldiers or the former leaders of the nationalist associations, which had been banned in Kenya during the war. The position was further complicated by a large minority of European settlers who were highly articulate, accustomed to self-government, and determined to secure its exercise for themselves. Prosperous Uganda, drawing its wealth from cotton and coffee, had no shortage of educated Africans, and African participation in government and commerce was assured. In Uganda, the problem was rather the position of the dominant Baganda minority and the position within the territory of the kabaka's court and the lukiko, against which riots broke out in 1945 and 1949. In all three mainland territories, however, discontent was smothered by the years of plenty which followed the war. Their revenue soared, owing to the inflated prices which were being paid for their primary produce. They also benefited from the Colonial Development and Welfare Act, passed in 1940, which made available £5 million a year for the development of British overseas dependencies.

East African high commission. Another important result of the Second World War was the creation of the East African high commission. Before the war there had been talk of closer union, and proposals to bring this about were discussed by the Hilton Young Commission and the Joint Select Committee on Closer Union, reference to which was made in the last chapter. When these proposals were discussed by a Joint Select Committe of both houses of parliament in England, it was decided that they were premature. At the same time, the three countries shared many problems which it was wasteful to consider separately. From 1926 onwards, therefore, there was always a conference, twice a year, between the governors of the three countries, together with the British Resident of Zanzibar. It had no authority, and its decisions could be carried out only after they had been referred to the various governments. During the Second World War the need for this co-operation was seen even more clearly, and it was agreed that an East African high commission should be set up, consisting of the governors of Kenya, Tanganyika and Uganda. At the same time, in 1948, the East African central legislative assembly was created to provide a means of discussion of the common interests of the three territories. As first proposed it gave equal representation to all three races as regards unofficials, but this was later modified in response to European pressure. The assembly met two or three times a year, in each of the territories in turn, and its membership was increased from twenty-three in 1948 to thirty-three in 1956, although only nine of these members were elected. The services controlled by the high commission included the East African railways and harbours, the posts and telecommunications, customs, research, and income-tax.

The East African common services organisation. The benefits which co-operation brought made Tanganyika anxious that it should continue when independence came. Therefore, after a conference in London and an investigation by the Raisman Commission, the high commission was reconstituted, in December 1961, as the East African common services organisation. In this organisation responsibility was to rest with the principal elected ministers of the three countries, who were the East African common services authority. The authority was to be supported by four groups: one for communications, one for finance, one for commerce and industry, and one for social and research services. There were to be three ministers in each group, one from each country.

After independence it was decided that this organisation did not go far enough in looking after the common interests of the three East African nations. In 1967 a treaty was, therefore, signed between them setting up an East African community, or common market. Under its terms, the three countries have the same external customs-duties; agricultural products are free from internal tariffs and surcharges on the internal trade in some industrial goods may only be imposed for a limited time. There is to be free exchange of currency at par between members of the community, and an East African development bank has been set up. Changes were also made in organisation. The East African legislative assembly now consists of three ministers (three deputy ministers may also be appointed), seven members chosen by each government, a chairman, the secretary-general and the law officer (the last two cannot vote at meetings).

Other economic and social developments. From 1945 onwards it became increasingly clear that East Africa was determined to secure independence. In the economic and social spheres marked characteristics were the development of communications, which was linked with the growing industrialisation, the drift to the towns and the remarkable growth of population. Roads are an important part of a country's communications and here much has been done, particularly in the tarmacing of main roads, like the one from Nairobi to Mombasa. In 1948 the railways amalgamated to form the East African Railways and Harbours Corporation and this made further extensions possible. In 1932 the first regular air service to England began, and in 1946 the East African Airways started internal flights and soon developed connections overseas. When Embakasi airport was finished in 1968 it became possible for jet-aircraft to land at Nairobi.

Approaching independence and the changes listed above strengthened the demand for better educational and health facilities. Details about their development are given under the separate sections in which the history of each of the four nations is outlined. At this point, however, it is worth mentioning that the content of education was increasingly looked at in an African setting.

KENYA

Final bid for white settler-control. As a country producing vitally needed food-stuffs, Kenya flourished at the end of the war, especially as she could now draw on capital and people who turned, with the withdrawal of Britain from India, to Kenya. European efforts to establish a dominant position in the colony were at first based on their economic contribution. This claim was, however, rejected by the Moyne report of 1932, which stated that 'In Kenya the prevailing bias had been towards the convenience of a civilization in which the native so far shares little of direct advantage.' The next European plan, based on closer union, has already been described. Finally, in 1948, the establishment for the first time of an unofficial majority in the legislative council provided an opportunity for the advance to self-government of a multi-racial state led by Europeans. At this time, however, few Europeans saw a future as members of a multi-racial community with equal rights, and African political developments were increasingly outside the legislative chamber. Then came Mau-Mau, which forced both the British government and the people of Kenya to think again about the future government of the colony.

A new way of life. Economic advances which looked good to Europeans had brought suffering to many Africans. In the early days of the twentieth century, primitive conditions restricted the increase of people and animals. The slave-trade, moreover, took a heavy toll of life, and epidemics which ravaged the country at the end of the century have been referred to. By the beginning of the twentieth century the slave-trade and slavery had been abolished, tribal warfare stopped and European medical and veterinary techniques were being introduced. Thus the death-rate decreased and the population rose; this increased the pressure on the land. In addition, certain land was subjected to increased pressure owing to the introduction of cash crops and the change from barter to cash systems of transaction. These changes made it difficult to follow the old system of moving from place to place to rest the land. Villagers were beginning to live in a world which had no contact with the past. In the last fifty years new ways of life had been opened in employment in government service, in forestry, on European farms, in towns and in the competitive worlds of commerce and industry. These occupations required skills and knowledge for which the young showed their aptitude in schools and colleges, and which their elders, by tradition the wise men of the people, were too old to acquire. Old men had moved through life as members of an age-set which was a unit; as such they had served first as warriors, next as junior elders and later as elders in power. Within the age-set, individuals were equal, although in some peoples there was provision for the rapid promotion of men of promise. If individuals in an age-set are equal, they have as much right to the vote as others in their group. The slogan 'one man, one vote' appealed, therefore, very strongly to the great majority of the nation who had not yet got the franchise.

Problems created by social change. Approximately one-quarter of the African population of Kenya belong to the Luo and Luyia peoples. The next largest group are the Kikuyu, who are approximately one-fifth of the total; a further one-tenth belong to their kindred peoples, the Meru and Embu. They live close to Nairobi, where the problems of an industrial society were particularly difficult. An increasing number of Africans had come to get jobs in the towns. These men were faced with many problems. Few were able to bring their families with them, and many found they had lost a sense of security. It is usually only skilled labour that commands good wages, and these men found themselves with very little money. When Africans began to spend longer periods in towns a serious situation arose. For one thing housing-schemes had failed to keep up with the increasing population.

By 1952 the drift to the towns had reached the proportions which history indicates cannot be checked by government action. During the industrial revolution England went through similar sufferings, and although problems that have occurred in the past may be better understood when they appear again today, it is not always easy to solve them.

At one time it was estimated that there were 10,000 unemployed Africans in Kenya, out of an African population which, in 1948, was reckoned to be five and a quarter million. Many of these were disappointed because they had either sought education and been unable to obtain it, or obtained it and found it did not lead to the kind of job they had hoped for; most of the junior technical and clerical posts in commerce, industry and the government were held by Asians. In 1947, in reply to a question in the legislative council, it was stated that the government and the railway between them paid salaries of Shs. 300 a month or more to only nine Africans.

The racial discrimination which checked Kikuyu economic, social and political ambitions showed itself in such ways as the restrictions on the planting of cash crops, like coffee, and the acquisition of land in the White Highlands, as well as in difference in wages.

Some Europeans understood these difficulties but did not realise their full significance to the Africans, whose real needs were not met by the paternalism which many of the Europeans showed. And many Africans thought Europeans treated them as inferiors, depriving them of their land and making them work on other men's farms. It was the Kikuyu who had come into closest contact with Europeans and their way of life; and they turned to the concept of tribal unity, making a show of reverence for their god, Ngai, and their ancestors, Gikuyu and Mumbi. Leaders in African society without indigenous chiefs are not elected but appear to come to the front supported by their group as a whole. They are usually gifted speakers, and men of ability, who hold views not very different from those of the group they lead.

K.A.U. After Harry Thuku's deportation the Young Kikuyu Association had been renamed the Kikuyu Central Association (K.C.A.) and revitalised. It held large meetings in the reserves, and owed much of its success to its general secretary Johnstone (later Jomo) Kenyatta. Linked with the K.C.A. was the Independent Schools Association, which stressed the teaching of English rather than Swahili and aimed at substituting an indigenous system of education for the mission schools. These were particularly unpopular at the time because of their opposition to female circumcision. The standard in the training-colleges, which were controlled by the missions, was often low, and an attempt to remedy this was made by Peter Koinange, who founded a teachers' training-college at Githunguri.

During the war the K.C.A. and other associations formed among the Kamba and the Taita were suppressed, but the return of African soldiers brought a revival of political activity; and in 1944 Mathu helped found the Kenya African Union (K.A.U.) to press for increased African membership of the legislative council, as a step towards African self-government. The members also demanded equal racial representation in the East African central assembly, better educational facilities, more land for Africans, and an end to the Kipande system. These aims were inconsistent with a European-dominated Kenya, but they were not revolutionary, and were shared by all Africans; hence the name Kenya African Union, which had been chosen to stress its national, rather than tribal, character.

Jomo Kenyatta. In 1946 Kenyatta returned from England, where he had been studying for a postgraduate diploma in anthropology at London

University and had published a book called *Facing Mount Kenya*. His name by this time was known throughout Kenya. He had been general secretary of the Kikuyu Central Association and been chosen as a spokesman on the land question before the Carter Commission of 1933, and was widely known as a brilliant orator. Outside East Africa he was known as a leader at the Pan African Conference held at Manchester in 1945. With this reputation he was given a tremendous welcome on his return to Kenya, but the governor could only suggest that he should start his political career at the bottom, taking part in local government. Within the year, however, he was president of the K.A.U. and principal of Githunguri training-college. These were influential positions in which he had a great deal to do with the 1940 group of Kikuyu. This was the name given to the group, many of whom had served in the army, who were circumcised in that year, and whose turn had come to take over the leadership of their tribe. Kenyatta's influence was shown at a large meeting held under his chairmanship, which resolved that women should not take any part in the terracing needed to check erosion: next day no women appeared.

A state of emergency. For some time there had been references to a new movement, Mau-Mau. The government was slow to admit its existence, and was also reluctant to recognise the strength of the demands of African nationalism. Mau-Mau was in the direct line of descent from previous Kikuyu political societies, and was first recognised officially under the name of Mau-Mau in 1949. It appeared to be a spearhead force for those who believed in the need for violence. In its early stages the new organisation bound itself together by oaths. By 1952 it had been forced underground and increasing numbers of Kikuyu had been bound up with it, some as a result of threats. Those who refused were, in many instances, killed. There is a story that an African who had served his European employer for many years was forced to take an oath that he would kill her. His genuine devotion to her and his genuine respect for the oath he found irreconcilable, so he committed suicide by drowning himself. Despite the growing crime-wave in Nairobi, the government hoped that the situation was not as serious as it seemed. Then, in October 1952, Chief Waruhiu was murdered in broad daylight, and the new governor, Sir Evelyn Baring, declared a state of emergency. Kenyatta, with other suspects, was detained and later tried with five others and convicted of managing Mau-Mau.

The struggle that followed was mainly confined to the region of the Aberdares and Mount Kenya and to the Nairobi district; it centred on the land. Kikuyu condemned to death would strive to scratch up a little earth in their prison cell and hold it out, when bravely facing their end, saying, 'For this I die.' On the other hand, many, but not all, Christians refused to take the oaths, claiming, like the early martyrs in Rome, that they were already bound to their God; and in so doing died for their faith. Many of the old people also rejected this perversion of the old ways.

At the beginning of the emergency Nairobi was the headquarters of the Mau-Mau movement, but by 1956 the city was cleared. The last struggles of the movement were in the Aberdares and on the slopes of Mount Kenya, where it is generally held to have ended in 1956 with the capture of Dedan Kimathi, who had become the real leader of the militant movement. By the time it ended 68 Europeans and more than 9,000 Africans, on both sides, had been killed; some were burnt alive, others were tortured. Nor were Mau-Mau attacks restricted to men; women and children, contrary to tribal custom, were included. Asians also were involved – 26 Asian civilians were killed, mostly in Nairobi. The state of emergency was not declared at an end till January 1960.

After the emergency. During the time of Mau-Mau isolated huts were fired and families slaughtered. In order to protect their supporters and prevent the gangs from commandeering supplies they needed, the government compelled the Kikuyu to live in villages under strict discipline and to farm their lands under supervision. By 1957 it was possible to develop what had been little more than labour lines as villages where social services, piped water and so on, which could not be provided for isolated land-holdings, were available. Closer administration was also possible, as the villages were near the road and, therefore, easier to reach. Many of these villages have become permanent towns for those with very little land; at the same time a large number have been abolished to enable the inhabitants to go and live on their consolidated farms. By 1960 the Kikuyu were able to return to Nairobi, from which most of them had been excluded. Although great efforts had been made to increase and improve the accommodation available, it was strained by the influx that ensued. The problems of the capital, though, were dwarfed by those of Kenya itself: social services had to be expanded, and the productivity of the land increased to pay for them, yet Kenya now had a public debt of £47 million as compared with the £16 million pounds owed by Tanganyika.

Since the war African agriculturalists have taken a much greater interest in the production of export crops. In 1952, for example, Africans sold three times as much wattle-bark as Europeans. In 1954 the British government was anxious to end the Mau-Mau rising, and made a grant of £5 million to intensify agricultural production in the African areas.

Swynnerton, an agricultural administrator, used it to engage specialist staff, to purchase equipment and to introduce special training and investigation-centres for agricultural, veterinary, forest and water development. This large investment, coupled with widespread land consolidation and enclosure, greatly increased the production of tea, coffee, pyrethrum, rice, cereals, sisal and animal products in the African areas. In the opinion of a recent mission by an international bank the results were unique, and stand as a model for future development in other countries besides Kenya.

Land tenure. In 1955 a royal commission was appointed to make recommendations, with reference to the economic development of the land and industrial activities in East Africa. It outlined the problem of land tenures as follows:

> The African way of life and sense of security have always been bound up in the land and his stock. Memories of famine deter him from changing his way of life until the success of the new ways has been demonstrated. Most land is held on customary tenure and farmed accordingly. In the last two decades this type of land tenure has shown itself to be ill-adapted to modern conditions.

On the coast customary land tenure had come under Arab influence, and individual rights to land were, therefore, recognised. Inland customary land tenure still prevailed. Among the good things that came out of the Mau-Mau rising was the opportunity to consolidate the fragmented holdings of the Kikuyu. Some owners of three or four acres had their land scattered in twenty different places, yet suggestions of land consolidation and individual titles to land were regarded with suspicion. Africans, especially those from Nyanza, felt that a handicapped class of landless men might be created, as they were in England by the agricultural revolution there. On the other hand, the agricultural changes in the England of the eighteenth century had helped the country to feed a rapidly rising population, which was absorbed in the growing towns by the industrial revolution. Kenya also had the problems of a rapidly rising population: in 1948 it was 5,505,966; by 1962 it had increased to 8,636,263.

By 1957 many people in the Kikuyu districts had come to understand the immense economic advantages of land consolidation and individual tenure of land. As a result the process of registration and consolidation was greatly speeded up, and spread to Nyanza province. At the same time there was a steady increase in land registration in such districts as Kipsigis, Nandi and Elgeyo; but in 1964 the Kamba were still reluctant to consolidate their land. This immense revolution in land tenure was recognised by the Kenya legislative council, which introduced proposals to make sure that the important considerations governing the ownership or occupation of land in the Highlands should only be those of the economic use of land, sound agricultural development and good husbandry, and not those of race.

Settlement schemes. In 1960 settlement schemes were introduced to help Africans to purchase and develop land in the scheduled areas which had previously been restricted to Europeans. Only part of the former 'White Highlands' was subject to the scheme, the areas round Kitale and Nakuru being excluded for the first five years so that they might continue to produce grain and dairy products to feed the non-farming population. In 1962 the government said that there would be a big extension of the small-holder scheme for those with little money. Within five years more than 50,000 families were settled on the land. At the same time the nation's production of cash crops like pyrethrum, tea and cotton went up; coffee remained stable. The really big increase, though, was in the sales of cattle, and the production of wheat, maize and pulses. Efficient production was most important, for agriculture still provided between eighty-five and ninety per cent of the money earned for Kenya by exports. Moreover about eighty per cent of the Kenyan citizens worked on the land (since independence non-citizens have not been allowed to buy land in Kenya), and their standard of living depended on efficient production. Therefore, when the small-holder scheme was revised in 1962, and it was known that the cost would be between £13 and £18 million, this was contributed in the form of loans and grants by Britain. It was Britain who provided a large part of the cost of the original scheme.

Post-war industrial development. Although Kenya's wealth is always likely to be in agriculture, manufacturers are growing in importance. During the years 1954–62, manufactured goods increased, and their value rose from £14·1 million to £23 million. The biggest increase took place in the textile industry, which makes Nakuru blankets and similar goods. This industry produced so much that its goods went up in value by 430 per cent. Matches, brewing, bricks, plastics and metal boxes are also among Kenya's developing industries. Some of these already produce nearly all the articles required by the local market – cigarettes and cement, for example. Construction industries, such as woodwork, have also developed. Industrial development is dependent on communications, and the 100 per cent increase in bitumen road surface between 1959 and 1963 is significant. Road travel grew and African-driven private cars became a familiar sight, although an African woman at the wheel still attracted some attention. Then there is the industry connected with garages; this, too, is going ahead.

In 1945 there were very few Africans in the retail trade. By 1963 their numbers had grown considerably and they were fast replacing the Asians, who once had a monopoly. Finally, all races are finding that the development of air and motor travel has changed their lives. Now that adequate transport services are available tourists are coming to the country in increasing numbers. In 1958 the director of external traffic at Nairobi and Mombasa Airports handled 45,965 passengers. By 1963 this number had risen to 90,640. Tourism was a valuable source of income to the Kenya of 1964 with a tremendous potential, and was looked after by a minister, who was also responsible for information and broadcasting. Travel means an increasing demand for petrol and oil. The opening of a large oil-refinery near Mombasa in 1963 was, therefore, an important event: Kenya had a new source of revenue and employment, and an asset worth millions of pounds.

Local history – Mombasa. Although Nairobi led the way in becoming a city, the oldest town in Kenya is, of course, Mombasa; its early history has already been described. A glance at the number of mosques shows that it remained a Muslim centre in the middle of the twentieth century. Here Asian and Arab traders lived in the old town, which was already outgrowing Mombasa island proper. The island is now linked to the mainland by Makupa causeway, Nyali bridge and a system of ferries.

Until 1926 Mombasa was only an anchorage port, but in that year the first deep-water berth was constructed at Kilindini, and by the early sixties Mombasa had thirteen others and was the leading seaport in East Africa. Its labour troubles, moreover, underlined the country's urban problems. The K.C.A. and the labour trades union of East Africa organised a strike in 1939 which led to an official enquiry, which showed that relatively good wages were attracting more men than there were jobs, and those who were fortunate enough to get one usually found that their employers did not provide the housing required by the law. In 1955 Tom Mboya demonstrated that trades union organisation makes for greater efficiency than a disorganised labour force.

By 1960 Mombasa was a thriving modern town as well as the chief market for the region's agricultural products. Cement-making, lime-burning, coffee-curing and the manufacture of glass, coconut-oil and soap were among its industries, and in 1961 an oil-refinery was opened nearby.

A description of the island written in 1890 by C. W. Hobley gives an idea of the changes that have come over it in the last eighty years.

Its extent was very limited. There was a town wall ... Once outside the narrow lanes of the native town no roads other than narrow footpaths existed, even the path leading to Kilindini was only about four feet wide and passed through jungle the whole way. The jungle was infested with puff-adders ... Leopards roamed the town at night.

Changes in local government. While Mombasa was Kenya's only major port Nairobi was the only town of any size in the interior and since 1900 its affairs have been managed by a committee. In 1950 Nairobi had become a city, later Nakuru, Kisumu, Eldoret and Mombasa developed municipal councils with mayors. Nairobi thus continued to lead the group of developing townships, as she had ever since the railway headquarters had been transferred to her, as the growing capital of the colony. A more important step was taken in 1950, when the African district councils ordinance was passed, which gave these councils a position similar to those of the municipalities. The new councils were able to provide a variety of services. They could also pass by-laws, some of which would be binding on people of all races who lived in their area. In 1952 an effort was made to fill an important gap in this system, and an ordinance was passed which allowed districts in the scheduled areas to set up county councils. These corresponded roughly to the African district councils, and replaced the European district councils, which had been little more than glorified road boards. In 1955 a constitution was also given to the smaller African councils which proved very successful.

Constitutional advance. Before the state of emergency was officially at an end Oliver Lyttleton, the British colonial secretary at the time, had seen the need to grant Kenya fuller powers of self-government. The most important change he made was the introduction of a council of ministers, which became the chief instrument of government in Kenya.

Further changes were introduced by the next colonial secretary, who increased the number of Africans in the legislative council, so that for the first time Asian and African elected members outnumbered European elected members. In 1957 the first African elections were held in Kenya.

That year Ghana reached independence, and thus became the first African member of the Commonwealth to achieve the target which Britain had worked towards in her colonies. The Mau-Mau movement had focused attention on the demand for independence in Kenya also, and a conference was called at Lancaster House.

In January 1960 all the elected members of the legislative council, plus a small number of nominated members, were asked to a conference at Lancaster House in London, which drafted a new constitution.

Under this, the executive was to consist of a council of twelve ministers with an unofficial majority, and an Arab representative should have the right of attendance. No restrictions were, however, put on the governor's power to nominate ministers and members of the legislative council. Unofficial posts were to be filled on a racial basis.

The legislative council was to consist of sixty-five elected members; twenty of these seats were allotted on a racial basis. The sixty-five elected members would then proceed to elect a further twelve members on a racial quota. The governor retained the right to nominate members.

Judges were to continue to be appointed by the governor.

Between conferences at Lancaster House. The absence of political parties had long been a characteristic of political life in Kenya. Candidates stood as individuals and not as members of parties. Shortly before the first Lancaster House conference, though, a multi-racial party, the New Kenya Group, had been formed under the leadership of Sir Michael Blundell; this was opposed by the United Party with its European supporters. After the conference the ban on country-wide African political parties was removed. Both the Kenya African National Union (commonly known as K.A.N.U.) and the Kenya African Democratic Union (usually known as K.A.D.U.) were now registered. The 1961 election was, therefore, a keenly-fought contest on party lines. When this was over the 'caretaker' government under the leadership of Mr Ngala, who had acted as spokesman for the African elected members at Lancaster House, resigned.

In the 1961 election a large number of independents were returned; but it was clear that K.A.N.U., with eighteen supporters, had defeated K.A.D.U., with only eleven. Mr Mboya was therefore asked to form a government, but refused until the real leader of the country, Kenyatta, was released. K.A.D.U. then agreed to accept office, and held it until 1962, when a second conference was held at Lancaster House. This was attended by Kenyatta, now released through pressure by African members. After a further short period of coalition government elections were held; as a result of these Mzee Jomo Kenyatta (as he now became known) became prime minister and Mr Ngala leader of the opposition.

Independence. After the second Lancaster House conference, the pace of the advance to independence increased rapidly, and a 'crash programme' of Africanisation of the administration was introduced. On 12 December 1963 Kenya became an independent country, and chose to remain within the British Commonwealth.

In August 1964 it was announced that Kenya would become a

republic on the first anniversary of independence. A day earlier the prime minister, in his capacity as president of the Kenya African Nation Union, had announced, 'From now on we will work toward a one-party state.' The essence of democracy is the rule of law and respect for individuals. In so far as it means the right of every man to be heard, this is a basic concept in East African thought. In the old days, in an African meeting both sides of an argument would be heard, but the final result was expected to be accepted unanimously. In this it differs from the two-party system of 'Westminster' democracy.

Fig. 7   Eight years after independence Kenyatta celebrates a rally in Nairobi

Post-war social development. Since the end of the Second World War in 1945, there has been a shift from mission control of social services to government control. This is shown in the increase (from 7,068 in 1953 to 10,617 in 1962) in the number of beds in government hospitals. It shows also in the growth of government schools. In addition the government has developed a network of health-centres and rural clinics. Youth clubs have been sponsored and community development schemes introduced. One of the most successful of these schemes was at Machakos, where by 1958 the whole district was included. Adult education was encouraged and courses held for African leaders which were open to both men and women. A Kenya Institute of Administration was also founded in 1961 to train senior civil servants as part of the Africanisation programme. By 1958 there were over 30,000 members of women's clubs in Kenya, and there are many more today. The Kenya women's seminary is another sign of the growing part women are playing in the public life of the country, and today many African women hold important posts. Again, in the 1961 election men were surprised by the enthusiasm with which the women voted. Eight years later, in the election held at the end of 1969, Mrs Grace Onyango became the first African woman to be elected to the

Fig. 8   President Kenyatta

Kenyan parliament; she has been joined by Mrs Jemimah Gecaga, who was included by the president in the list of twelve nominated members who represent special interests.

A changing way of life has led to the spread of dress and customs that are common overseas among the younger people; there are examples of this in housing and furniture. Ways of eating have also altered. An increasing number of Africans go to hotels and restaurants when travelling. Many women have more to do in their homes, which gives less time for their work on the land. Changes are likely to increase now that many more girls go to secondary schools; especially as the young, both men and women, have greater opportunities to travel beyond the boundaries of Kenya. Within the country cars and motor bicycles now carry their owners to areas that were once far beyond their reach. The older people have also benefited from adult literacy campaigns and the effects of broadcasting and television (the latter was introduced in 1962). Changing interests are shown in the figures of books borrowed from the East African postal library service, which now lends over twice as high a proportion of fiction as it did in 1954.

Another important feature has been the spread of trade unionism among African industrial workers and of co-operative societies among farmers. Wages have risen substantially since the Carpenter Report advocated that African urban wages should be adequate to support a family, and not just a single man. This report was followed by the introduction of the Lidbury scales of pay in the civil service, when it was announced that salaries would be based on the work done and not on the race of the person doing it. On the other hand there is a growing number of unemployed, partly due to the drift to towns away from rural areas, where a traditional way of life once provided occupation for all the members of society. Three out of four adult men still earn their living from the land, and the 1969 census showed that only 10 per cent of the population are town-dwellers. A substantial number of these live in Nairobi. The population of the city was calculated as 118,976 in 1948, by 1962 it had risen to 243,000 and and is now at least 477,600.

This, however, is only part of the picture; the population is increasing at the alarming rate of 3·3 per cent per annum. This is a figure which it would have been almost impossible to provide for in the economy before 1945. The number of Africans attending primary school is also increasing rapidly. Between 1953 and 1962 it roughly doubled, and seven years' primary education for all boys was in sight. School-leavers find it hard to get a job, and there is heavy unemployment among them. At the same time only about 12 per cent of those completing the primary school are able to go on to secondary schooling, despite the startling increase in the number of schools provided, which has risen from 19,239 in 1959 to 101,361 in 1968. Higher school certificate classes were started in African schools in 1961, and since then, the number of entrants has increased very substantially; yet there is an acute shortage of teachers with university degrees. Part of the demand for further education is met at the University College, which was founded as a multi-racial institution. Fifteen years earlier a multi-racial college would have seemed impracticable, but the old distinctions are becoming blurred and single-race schools (secondary ones at any rate) seem an anachronism today. In *Facing Mount Kenya*, Kenyatta pointed out that to the Europeans 'the individual is the ideal of life, to the Africans the ideal is the right relations with and behaviour to other people'. Today this distinction also is less marked. The training of technicians and skilled craftsmen is very important as well, being closely linked with the economic development of a country. In the last few years the old European Egerton College has become the multi-racial Kenya Forest School, and farmers training centres have been established; while technical and commercial education have been developed in the Kenya Polytechnic.

Health services. Early hospital treatment depended substantially on the missions, and even today 30 per cent of all hospital beds in Kenya and 40 per cent of all actual hospitals are still under church management. There are approximately a total of 140 hospitals and the government aim is to establish a hospital of 200 beds in every district. All hospitals are now multi-racial; child patients are admitted free, adults pay a flat rate of ten shillings on admission.

Special developments include the introduction, since independence, of radio-therapy in Nairobi; this is probably the first unit to be installed north of the Limpopo. There are two other remarkable examples of self-help in action. One of these is President Kenyatta's own hospital project. The other is the Presbyterian Church's Chagoria hospital for which a quarter of a million pounds was raised – £80,000 being contributed by the people of Meru districts themselves.

UGANDA

Economic development. In 1939 society in Uganda could still be described as static, despite the cash crops, such as cotton and sugar, which had been added to the traditional peasant economy and brought in money for extras. Then the Second World War came, and 55,000 Ugandans were conscripted. In the second half of the war the stress was on agricultural production; maize production was doubled and the export of cotton increased one hundred per cent. The remarkable rise in cotton prices after the war made it an increasingly popular crop with the Baganda; they were discouraged by the government's marketing policy, which depressed the price paid to the cotton-grower.

During the early 1950s the crop brought in £11–£12 million annually, and today Uganda is the greatest coffee-producer in the Commonwealth. By far the greatest part of the crop is of the Robusta variety. Again, production is encouraged and controlled by the government.

Another development plan. By 1961, when a further five year plan was drawn up, over seven per cent of the total domestic product was being spent on social services. Although Uganda was at the time a relatively prosperous African country this is a high percentage; according to Elkan in *The Economic Development of Uganda* even the United States does not spend a very much higher percentage. In the five year development plan it was clearly recognised that Uganda was an agricultural country, with ninety per cent of all her exports coming from the land. It was also recognised that coffee and cotton were 'the most important factors in deciding the size of the national income', as they alone accounted for over sixty per cent of Uganda's export earnings. Sugar, sisal, groundnuts, tea and livestock account for most of the remaining agricultural produce.

In this connection the following table taken from *Zamani*, edited by B. A. Ogot and J. A. Kieran, is useful.

Foreign Trade and Government Revenue 1911 to 1961: Uganda

	Exports (£m)	Imports (£m)	Government Revenue (£m)	Main Export Commodities as % of total exports	
				Cotton	Coffee
1911	0·3	0·5	0·2	55	1
1921	1·5	not available	0·8	85	6
1931	1·9	1·3	1·4	84	8
1951	47·4	22·1	15·8	62	29
1961	46·0	24·5	22·3	43	36

Marketing policy. In 1937 Uganda's total revenue was just under £2 million of which about £100,000 was being spent annually on education and about twice as much went on medical services. The smallness of the revenue was a result of the low prices raw materials were fetching in the world markets, and it handicapped the development of the public services.

In 1942 a rise in the world prices of cotton and coffee changed the position: these crops were already producing £41·6 millions a year and could have produced more but for the government marketing policy. Marketing boards were established, which were given a monopoly over the export of cotton and coffee. These boards acted on the false assumption that word-market prices would fall, and it would be necessary, therefore, to build up reserves in order to be able to pay a reasonable price to the growers when this inevitably happened. As there was nothing inevitable about it, and prices did not fall, the boards accumulated huge funds; in 1954 they had £37 million. This was because they were paying growers less than the market price. By the time it was clear that prices were not likely to fall the boards had become concerned about the danger of inflation. They considered this would come about if they paid out funds which would be spent on imported goods. Here, too, the danger was exaggerated, as transport difficulties and world-wide shortages would anyhow have checked the temptation to import on a substantially larger scale. Although it cannot be proved, it is possible that higher prices would both have encouraged new enterprises and increased the total production of cotton. But it must be remembered that there was another reason why cotton-growing, apart from that in some districts of the Northern and Eastern Provinces, did not expand in the post-war years: coffee, in those parts where it could be grown, was a more profitable crop. Before leaving the part played by the government in the economy, the establishment of the Uganda Development Corporation in 1952 should be mentioned. It was given a capital of £5 million, to enable it to stimulate more businesses and encourage overseas investment, and has had a moderate success. One other factor besides agriculture must be mentioned in connection with Uganda's economy.

Hydro-electric power. The other factor which should be mentioned is the Owen Falls Hydro-electric Scheme. It was Sir Winston Churchill who wrote in 1907 that 'It would be perfectly easy to let the Nile begin its long and beneficent journey to the sea by leaping through a turbine.' In 1954 his statement became a reality when the British queen opened the great dam built across the Nile at Jinja. The electrical power from the Owen Falls is carried to Kenya as well as Uganda, and has made possible the establishment of further industries.

The development of central and local government. After the Second World War the legislative council became a focus of political and national advance. In 1945 Africans were represented for the first time, and the council was reorganised with an equal number of official and unofficial members, beside the governor, whose vote gave the government side a majority. After being enlarged twice, in 1950 African representation was made equal to that of the Asian and European unofficials combined.

Local government was based on the division of the country into four provinces (Buganda Province, Northern Province, Eastern Province, Western Province), which were subdivided into districts. Although the constitutional position varied between the 'agreement' kingdoms and other parts of Uganda, a general pattern of local government developed, with the executive powers carried by the provincial commissioners, district commissioners, and chiefs, assisted by advisory councils. The main characteristics of development were the increasing responsibility given to the local authorities and the increasing degree of election to their councils.

Local government also developed in the towns. In 1958 Kampala and Jinja, the two largest, were given municipal councils with power to levy rates and administer their own social services. At the same time Mbalo and Masaka, which were next in size, were given town councils, while the remaining towns were administered by town boards.

The kabaka crisis. The policy of indirect rule which Britain followed in Uganda meant that the position of the traditional rulers, i.e. kings and chiefs, had been strengthened. There was a conflict, therefore, between a dawning nationalism and traditional interests. The members of a feudal society were afraid both of being ruled and of having their traditional social life disturbed by imperialism. Sir Andrew Cohen, who became governor in 1952, was determined to democratise the government and made further complicated changes in the composition of the legislative council. These changes gave Africans more influence over their government than they had anywhere else, in either Tanganyika or Kenya. What they lacked was direct elections, based on constituencies, to a legislative council which represented the whole country, and it did not seem as if the country wanted to make this further advance. The lukiko was afraid that if it nominated members to the legislative council that body would claim that it was genuinely representative of the whole protectorate. There was also a lurking fear – not so real, but haunting East African history – that federation with other East African countries would be enforced, leading to domination by Kenya. It so happened that a chance remark on this topic by the colonial secretary in 1953 provoked a major collision between the Buganda and protectorate governemnts.

It was unfortunate that circumstances should have forced two such men as the governor and the kabaka into political collision, for both were sincerely anxious to promote the interests of the African people.

The Kabaka Mutesa II, who had succeeded Daudi Chwa in 1942 at the age of eighteen, had been one of the first to welcome the appointment of Sir Andrew, for they were old friends. Edward Mutesa himself was no illiterate despot but a Cambridge graduate and an ex-officer of the Guards regiment in the British army, faced with a powerful lukiko. Nevertheless, when the fears of an East African federation were revived in 1953 he decided to support his ministers and the lukiko in demanding, among other things, that the federation issue should be dropped, and that Buganda should become independent within 'a short, stated, space of time'. Sir Andrew, after consultation with the colonial secretary gave a speedy assurance that a policy of federation would not be followed, but he refused to grant the request for immediate independence, which was considered impractical; for Uganda had always been developed as a united territory, whose main centres – Kampala and Entebbe – were situated in Buganda, which had between a third and a quarter of the total population. The kabaka, in accordance with the 1900 agreement, was expected by the governor to support these views in the lukiko. The lukiko stated later that 'If he had chosen to do the Governor's bidding, we, the Lukiko, would have expelled him.' As it was, the kabaka refused to comply, and announced his intention to oppose the governor's decisions publicly and to advise the lukiko to reject them. After persistent attempts to compromise had failed, recognition was withdrawn from him by the British government in November 1953. He was deported to Britain, and became a hero overnight to the Baganda.

The 1955 Buganda agreement. The deadlock was ended by an agreement that Buganda should remain an integral part of the protectorate of Uganda, and that the kabaka himself should become a constitutional monarch retaining the right to sign laws passed by the lukiko, although ministers were to be responsible for every act. Further constitutional changes included the introduction of a ministerial system and the agreement of the lukiko committee to Buganda representatives sitting in the legislative council, on the understanding that no further constitutional changes would be made until 1961.

Baganda's obstructions. The temporary harmony on constitutional advance was disturbed when Buganda refused to take part in the elections for the legislative council of 1957. Again the basic reason was that the Buganda leaders feared that their own kingdom and authority would be swamped by the growing power of the legislative council and protectorate, but the occasion of their protest was the appointment of a speaker, instead of the governor, as chairman of the council. This, claimed the Baganda, was a breach of the agreement to avoid constitutional changes until 1961. However, despite the lack of co-operation from Buganda, elections were held in 1958, and the experiment of direct elections proved generally popular.

In 1959, while Buganda was still troubled by disturbances, and while the African parties of the protectorate agitated increasingly for political independence, the government appointed a committee to suggest the constitutional developments which should follow the end of the time-pause in 1961. The committee recommended that the 1961 legislative council should be renamed the national assembly and should have an overwhelming majority of African members that were directly elected. It also recommended that the executive council should be appointed mainly from the elected members of the legislative council. Most of the people in Uganda welcomed these suggestions, and accordingly elections were held in March 1961. These were won by the Democratic Party led by Mr Benedicto Kiwanuka, who became chief minister, while Dr Milton Obote, the leader of the Uganda People's Congress (U.P.C.), was recognised as leader of the opposition.

Buganda remained rigidly opposed to these constitutional changes. The 1961 elections were boycotted; the lukiko passed a resolution in favour of immediate secession; something had to be done.

Uganda becomes independent. In fact something had been done already, for a Relationships Committee had been appointed to suggest a solution to the Buganda problem, and in September 1961 its recommendations formed the basis for a constitutional conference in London. Here the long-awaited agreement was reached on a time-table for independence. Internal self-government was to begin in March 1962 and complete independence in October that year. The Buganda problem was settled by arranging that Buganda's relationship with the central government should be a federal one.

This time-table was kept, and Uganda thus became a constitutional monarchy with the British queen, represented by the governor-general, as head of state. By its constitution, Uganda was to consist of five federal states, ten administrative districts, and the territory of Mbale.

The supreme central legislature became the parliament of Uganda, consisting of the queen and the national assembly. This assembly had sixty-one members elected by universal adult suffrage, twenty-one representing Buganda, and nine elected by the assembly. Elections for a new assembly were normally to be held every five years.

Educational development. Some impression of the scale of development in education can be gained by glancing at the annual government grant. In 1925 the department of education had only £2,000; by 1960 the annual grant for education had risen to £5 million. In 1963–4 about 23 per cent of the national budget went on education.

Not only has the amount spent increased substantially, there has also been a change in organisation. From 1957 onwards the official policy has been to stress the integration of pupils of different races and religions;

previously there had been separate racial and religious education. Since 1961 there has also been a remarkable increase, nearly 300 per cent, in the number going on to secondary school. In the secondary schools themselves the decision by Makerere to take only students who had already obtained a higher certificate meant that in 1963 advanced level courses were run at fifteen senior secondary schools. Two other features in the educational development of Uganda should be noted; the increased facilities available outside Buganda, where they had previously been concentrated, and the expansion in girls' education. Further expansion is limited by the high cost per student; it takes about a £1,000 a year to keep a student at Makerere, and about £800 to build a pupil a place at a senior secondary school.

Health. Another major drive has been made to improve health; here missionaries played a prominent part. Foremost among them was Albert Cook, a distinguished surgeon and physician, who came out at the end of the nineteenth century and was knighted for his services in 1932. In 1897, when he founded Mengo hospital, it was built of reeds with a mud floor, and the outpatients were seen in a converted smithy which had been used as a dispensary. In his *Uganda Memories* Sir Albert tells how 'There was no operating theatre, or table, or hospital. The bad cases had to lie in the porch of the little dispensary, or in small huts run up for the occasion. The bottles for stock were the empty bottles in which the communion wine had come.' Mengo is one of the twenty-five mission hospitals; in 1969 there were thirty-one government and twenty-five mission hospitals. Mulago, a new teaching-hospital costing about £2,500,000, was opened at Kampala during the independence celebrations. The contrast between 1969 and 1897 also reflects the increased control of the country's affairs by the protectorate government, in which medical services were the foremost department. Today a ministry of social services integrates mission hospitals, district and sub-district hospitals and rural dispensaries, some of which have become health-centres in which the cure and prevention of disease are stressed.

TANGANYIKA

Post-war economic development. Before the Second World War investors regarded Tanganyika with caution, because they were not certain what its future would be if Hitler demanded the return of Germany's ex-colonies. This obstacle was cleared in 1946, when Britain agreed to it becoming a trust territory under the United Nations. By now improved communications were making it easier to deal with the ever-present threat of famine, which haunted the administration. This was in spite of the fact that Tanganyika's economy, like those of the other East African countries, is based on agriculture and livestock, which together provide eighty per cent of the exports. The most important crop since the beginning of the century has been sisal, which was introduced by the Germans, and since before the Second World War Tanganyika has been the world's greatest producer. As a plantation crop sisal requires a large capital outlay and easy access to communications, so it was chiefly developed by Asians and Europeans near the railways or the sea. But by 1960 cotton and coffee, which were grown almost entirely by small African farmers, were together nearly as valuable as sisal. Fourteen years earlier there had been an unfortunate interlude when the ground-nuts scheme was introduced on an ambitious scale by the British government, who hoped that it would encourage African prosperity and production in Tanganyika, while supplying the British housewife with the fats she wanted so badly. As speed was vital if votes were to be caught at the next British election, the local inhabitants were not consulted, precise rainfall measurements were not taken, and the soil was not tested. The result was a loss of £20 million to the British taxpayer.

In order to facilitate economic development in the south, especially in connection with the ground-nuts scheme, the Southern Province railway was constructed, and by 1954 had been opened to Nachingwea. Originally the railway began from Lindi, but when the new port of Mtwara was opened in 1954 that became the main outlet. By 1964 a line joining Ruvu to Korogwe at last made it possible to travel by rail from Dar es Salaam to Nairobi and Kampala, instead of having to use the steamer link across Lake Victoria. In 1961 plans for a Chinese loan to build a railway line to Zambia were accepted and the survey work has started.

Although Tanganyika is primarily an agricultural country, it has the most valuable mineral resources of any of the East African countries. Until the 1930s these were not seriously developed, but by the early 1960s they provided about thirteen per cent of the exports. At first gold was the most valuable mineral, but in 1940 Dr Williamson, a Canadian geologist, discovered an extremely rich diamond pipe near Shinyanga, and since then diamonds have become by far the most important mineral export. The most valuable stone yet discovered in the Shinyanga mine, valued at over £10,000, Dr Williamson gave to the British queen (then Princess Elizabeth) as a wedding present.

Development plans. The rapid economic development of Tanganyika has been due, in great measure, to the series of development plans. These have been financed partly by loans and partly by the British Colonial Development and Welfare Acts. One ten year plan was launched in 1947, and in 1961 another three-year plan was started. This was guided to some extent by the World Bank Mission. The planners came to the conclusion that the most urgent objective for Tanganyika's growth were the development of agriculture and livestock (and therefore of water-supplies as well); the improvement of communications; and the development of secondary and technical education. Measures to implement these decisions were taken, but those responsible emphasised that they would not bring a great increase in prosperity overnight; they were primarily laying the foundations for future growth.

Nationalist movements. After the end of the Second World War Tanganyika's output of cotton, coffee and sisal increased rapidly; coffee exports, for instance, earned £896,000 in 1945; ten years later their earnings had risen to £6,905,000. Tanganyika's farmers now organised themselves in co-operative societies, the leading members of which began to rival the chiefs in their influence. These new men were thinking on national lines. They found a nation-wide organisation, the Tanganyika African Association (to which reference was made at the beginning of this chapter) already established. Finally there was the unifying influence of Islam, which in the Kilimanjaro area had shown itself able to disregard the barriers formed by individual chiefdoms.

Julius Nyerere. The Tanganyika African Association and the Tanganyika African Civil Servants Association remained clubs rather then revolutionary organisations. But they were important because they provided central nationalist organisations which were in touch with tribal organisations like those founded by Kiiza among the Haya, to resist the chiefs. The turning-point came when Dr Nyerere returned to Tanganyika from his studies in Scotland; he was then only thirty-three. Although he was the son of a chief, he had had a hard childhood, but was lucky enough to have gone to Tabora school. Here he became a Roman Catholic, and his gifts convinced the headmaster that he must go on to a university. This meant Makerere, and later Edinburgh, from which he came back to Tanganyika to teach biology and history at St Mary's Catholic school, for £6 5s. a month, half the salary he would have got in a government school. Dr Nyerere was already determined to revive T.A.A. and joined the Tabora branch; from then on politics became increasingly important. Here he first called for freedom and unity, arguing that what the British did to the Germans in the Second World War could be done to the British by the Africans. At a meeting of T.A.A.

in 1953 Dr Nyerere persuaded the leaders to reorganise the association on the lines of Nkrumah's Convention People's Party.

T.A.N.U. The object of the new organisation, which was called the Tanganyika African National Union, (T.A.N.U.) was to prepare the people for self-government and independence. 'We mean to work towards self government in a constitutional manner', Dr Nyerere stated, at a meeting of the trusteeship council of the United Nations. The new organisations took over from T.A.A., which Dr Nyerere described as 'a semi-social and semi-political organisation'.

In Buhaya it penetrated the local branch of T.A.A. and took over the organisation, and in Chagga country it successfully outvoted the Kilimanjaro Union. By varying its tactics in this way T.A.N.U. expanded throughout the country.

Meanwhile, Dr Nyerere had carried the struggle to the United Nations. In 1954 T.A.N.U. had been accepted by a visiting United Nations mission as a nationalist movement, and Dr Nyerere went as its representative to New York, in 1955 and 1956. The obstacles he had to overcome, and the impression he made, are vividly described in *The Making of Tanganyika* by Judith Listowel. The impression he made on the governor, Sir Edward Twining, however, was that he was a dangerous young man who might frustrate the governor's plan. Twining thought that the preparation for independence, which had been promised when Tanganyika became a trust territory, would take a long time and involve the creation of a multi-racial government in which the chiefs would play a leading part, probably forming a second chamber. So Dr Nyerere's rejection of multi-racial government and demand for independence by a fixed date under an African government, seemed to him to threaten economic ruin to the country which would lose its expatriate civil servants and no longer attract foreign investors. It was not possible, however, to ignore Julius Nyerere after his success in New York, and in 1957 he was appointed a member of the legislative council; he found this so frustrating that he resigned shortly before the country's first general elections in 1958. By this time some 200,000 Africans had T.A.N.U. memberships cards, but the party had still to be persuaded by Dr Nyerere that it was essential that they should put up candidates in the 1958 election – this being the first general election ever to be held in Tanganyika – and not stand apart as a protest against the method of voting. The voting procedure had been devised with the object of involving all citizens in voting for all races. The result was an overwhelming triumph for Dr Nyerere in Tanganyika. By this time Twining had been replaced as governor by Turnbull, and relationships between government house and Dr Nyerere improved overnight. The path to independence was now a smooth one.

T.A.N.U. urged that the speed of advance towards self-government should be increased, and as this was the goal the government had always been working towards, and as Julius Nyerere – now the leader of T.A.N.U. – had widespread support and was able to co-operate on friendly terms with the governor, the next advance came in 1960, when a new and larger legislative council was created with, for the first time, a majority of elected members. Meanwhile the executive council had been replaced by a council of ministers. As Dr Nyerere's party won all the elected seats except one (his majority was certain before the election, as most of the T.A.N.U. candidates were unopposed) the governor asked him to be the chief minister, and choose ten of the fourteen members of the council of ministers. Tanganyika thus reached responsible government. Full independence came in December 1961. Mwalimu Nyerere (as he now called himself) then became the first prime minister, and the legislative council was renamed the national assembly. In December 1962 Tanganyika became a republic with Mwalimu Nyerere as president, but remained within the Commonwealth.

The Tanganyika constitution of 1962 laid down that the executive power of the republic should be vested in the president. His position was made elective, normally after five years, in order to correspond with the elections for each new national assembly. This assembly, together with the president, comprised the legislature of the republic. The national assembly was essentially, democratic, consisting of 107 members, elected by universal adult suffrage, with 1 member for each constituency, and with an electoral commission to ensure that the constituencies had roughly equal populations. On the other hand the president was given extensive powers, which included control over the armed forces and authority to choose his cabinet and to summon or dissolve parliament, besides the power to nominate up to ten members of the national assembly over and above those who were elected.

Chiefs and local government. In 1945 although the capital, Dar es Salaam, had a population of 67,000 it still had no municipal government. But in 1953 a Local Government Bill was passed introducing local councils at various levels, as a necessary development from the native authorities devised by Sir Donald Cameron. These new councils were given increased responsibilities, and a training-school giving courses on local government administration was started for chiefs and those recommended by the native authorities. Nevertheless, the pace of development in local government was slow in comparison with the extremely rapid advances on the national level, partly because there was no general agitation for it. Until 1961 local government was tied up with the chiefs. Their usual position in tribal society has been paralleled with that of princes and barons in mediaeval Europe. They commanded in war, judged criminals, enclosed the tribe's land and presided over the meetings, or *barazas,* usually held under a big tree, at which all members had the right to speak. Unlike European barons, or even princes, the chiefs also took the lead in religious ceremonies. The only restriction on these extensive powers used to be that of the elders, whose age and experience enabled them to bring considerable influence to bear. With the development of cash crops there appeared wealthy and well-educated Africans, who resented the power of the chiefs, and the foundation of the Tanganyika African National Union in 1954 was another challenge. For a time, the chiefs tried to bargain with the T.A.N.U. to secure recognition of their position, but the sweeping success of T.A.N.U. at the 1958 and 1959 elections left the chiefs with no bargaining power when Dr Nyerere informed them that he did not see any future for them in the local government of their country. Following independence the weight of responsibility in local government has moved increasingly towards regional councils supervised by T.A.N.U.

Education. By 1954 the percentage of primary-school children receiving education had risen 30 per cent, and illiteracy was being reduced at the rate of 2 per cent a year. Later the top of the educational ladder a sixth-form course leading to higher school certificate was started. By 1965 22 secondary schools had been founded, 10 with sixth forms leading to higher school certificate, and all secondary education was made free.

Meanwhile native-authority schools had been founded on Tabora lines. The teachers' salaries in these were financed by the native authorities, and all the teachers were Africans. There is a different source of finance for secondary schools, which are built to take in 10 per cent of those who pass out successfully from a full primary course. In 1963 56 per cent of the school-age population were in Standards 1–11, 43 per cent in Standards 3 and 4, 9 per cent in Standards 5 and 6 and 5 per cent in Standards 7 and 8. It is therefore only a minority of pupils who have the opportunity of completing a full primary school course.

Girls are at a further disadvantage. The first scheme for girls' boarding-schools, run by missionaries with the support of government grant-in-aid, was launched in 1929 at Tabora. It met with considerable opposition until Dr Makwaia, who was a powerful man in Shinyanga and a strict Muslim, sent both his eldest daughter and his favourite young wife there. Stress was at first laid on vocational training, housecraft in this instance, but in 1953 the school certificate was taken, and in 1960 three out of the four candidates who entered for the higher school certificate were successful. In 1962 all schools became national schools and racial divisions ended.

In 1965 the African population of Tanganyika was estimated as 10,046,000; in addition it was estimated that there were 111,500 Asians and Arabs and 17,300 Europeans. The vast majority of the Africans are peasant farmers and in 1962 only half a million were recorded as being in paid employment. Since 1920 the Chagga had found it more profitable to grow coffee than to go out for work, and their example was soon followed by the Haya. Of the remaining 120 tribes to be found in the country the Sukuma are the largest, the next being the Nyamwezi, Ha, Makonde, Gogo, Haya and Chagga; and employers depended mainly on the first four, and the southern tribes, for labour. Map 4 shows that the Nyamwezi, Ha, Makonde, Gogo and Sukuma live mainly on the highlands, the lakeside, and the coastal plain. In these regions most of them graze their cattle, cultivate their land and hope to produce enough food for themselves besides a small cash crop of cotton, coffee and ground-nuts. Some tribes, like the Maasai, are purely pastoral.

Standards of living. Under the German administration most of the Europeans in Tanganyika were Germans, but after the First World War all Germans were forced to leave and their properties were sold. In 1925 German settlers were allowed to return. Most of them were financed by the Usagara Company which was in practice an instrument controlled by the German government, and almost all the settlers were Nazis, so they were interned during the Second World War and later repatriated. At the time of independence there were only some 20,000 Europeans, of whom probably only a minority were British by origin. Those who wished to stay were allowed to assume citizenship under the Citizenship Bill which Nyerere persuaded T.A.N.U. to accept.

The Asian community has played an outstanding part in the country's economic life. They controlled the petty trade of Tanganyika for many years, and have had a major share in large commercial undertakings and been among the largest sisal-producers. In addition they became considerable land-owners, much of the land having been purchased from the Germans, who were forced to sell it after the First and Second World Wars. Since 1964 the Chinese have also begun to play a growing part in the life of Tanganyika, particularly in training the police and armed forces.

Standards of living have gradually improved; court-houses and schools are now usually built of stone or cement, and rectangular houses of latticed poles, plastered with mud, have mostly replaced rondavels. Village sanitation is found, and in 1940 the government appointed its first trained African doctor. Malaria, leprosy, blindness and yaws still remained major diseases; but now there were 20 major leprosariums, 250 hospitals and over 1,000 out-patients dispensaries.

At the time of independence diet still consisted of the traditional foods of millet, maize and rice and few imported goods were bought by the average family. Imported shoes were, however, becoming common, and more men wore shorts and white shirts. African small traders were also seen more frequently.

A new problem, however, was now faced by the administration, that of a growing gulf between the more prosperous wage-earners and the mass of the people. The president was keenly aware also of the danger of concentration on urban development. The Arusha Declaration, issued in 1967, pointed out that 'People who live in towns can possibly become exploiters of those who live in the rural areas. All our big hospitals are in towns ... Tarmac roads, too, are mostly found in towns and are of especial value to the motor-car owners.' It went on to say that 'The only road through which the country can be developed is by increasing agricultural development.'

ZANZIBAR

Constitutional development. The establishment of a legislative council in 1926 had provided Zanzibar with the means of further constitutional development. In this development, however, Britain was careful to see that the Arab community retained their privileged position. They, however, still looked back to the period when Zanzibar was an independent Arab island ruled by an Arab sultan, and were determined to throw off the British yoke. In 1956 a new constitution was introduced, which granted them their desire for elections on a common roll. Six of the twelve unofficial members in the new legislative council were to be elected. The Arab-dominated Zanzibar Nationalist party lost all six seats to the Afro-Shirazi party (most of the indigenous African population on the island call themselves Shirazi) and the weakness of the Arab position was exposed. By 1958 politics were absorbing the people of Zanzibar and the senior commissioner reported: 'Traders, cultivators, labourers, fishermen, even housewives were affected. Villagers in the rural areas argued among themselves. Funerals and religious ceremonies were boycotted by rival political parties!'

Events on the mainland seemed to have overtaken Zanzibar, and Sir

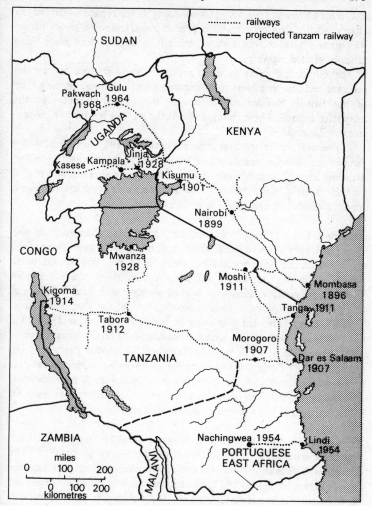

Map 16   Railways in East Africa

Hilary Blood was appointed to review the position. In his opinion 'A period of real ministerial responsibility, during which power in the Resident's hands will enable him to come to the rescue should anything go vitally wrong, is required before Zanzibar can complete the crossing of the great divide which separates the present non-representative from fully responsible government.'

Recommendations of the Blood Commission. In his recommendations Sir Hilary advised the creation of a predominantly elective legislature in which the official members should entirely disappear, their place being taken by elected members.

The bill giving effect to these proposals also arranged for a chief minister and four ministers to be appointed by the sultan, on the advice of the British Resident, from among the elected members of the legislative council. These changes meant the start of responsible government in Zanzibar.

In preparation for the first general election in 1961 to be held under the new constitution, the Zanzibar Nationalist Party appealed to fellow-Muslims among the indigenous Africans on the island. They also played on their distrust of the Africans who had come over from the mainland, many of whom belonged to the Afro-Shirazi party.

Elections. Until 1895 Pemba was left, as far as administration was concerned, very much to itself. Since then, it has had a large share of the amenities of the protectorate, but members of the Afro-Shirazi party who lived on the island were still not satisfied. Many of the Arabs on Pemba were small-holders, who worked together with local members of the Afro-Shirazi party to form a separate group, the Zanzibar Pemba People's Party. This led to a draw in the 1961 election, and a second election had to be held in which the boundaries of certain constituencies were drafted so as to favour the Zanzibar Nationalist Party and the Pemba People's Party. This coalition won eighteen out of thirty-one seats although a majority of the electors voted against it. A constitutional conference was held in London in 1962, and independence was given on 12 December 1963 to a government representing a minority.

Education. The last substantial improvement in boys' secondary education came with higher certificate courses introduced about 1959. The education of girls lagged behind, and a government secondary school for them was not started till 1947. Further extension of education depended on an increase in the material economy and a change in attitude towards the education of the large African population of the island, which was relatively neglected. The change came with the revolution of 1964. Schools were nationalised and education made free. It is, however, limited: the proportion of secondary to primary schooling remains static, although secondary school numbers have increased. Primary-school numbers have more than doubled; they were 3,000 in 1964, and rose to 7,500 in 1966.

CHAPTER 12

THE INDEPENDENT EAST AFRICAN
STATES 1964-1971

External relations. All three East African territories are members of the British Commonwealth, the United Nations Organisation and Organisation for African Unity. They oppose apartheid and support anti-colonial movements. They have also made it clear that they are not going to join either the Communist or the American bloc, and Mwalimu Nyerere has added that Tanzania 'will not allow her friends to choose her enemies'. In 1961 he also made it clear that Tanganyika would not join the British Commonwealth if South Africa with its policy of apartheid remained a member; South Africa withdrew.

The advantages of federation have again come to the front, now that it has no connection with the ambitions of a white minority. And under the 1967 Treaty for East African Co-operation, plans have been made to reverse the tendency to economic separation seen in the previous three to four years. In Kenya there was also a specific frontier problem, for Somalia became independent in 1960. And she then demanded a readjustment of the boundaries with Kenya, so that she might include the Somali, who lived in the Northern Frontier District. A series of *shifta*, or guerrilla, raids deep into Kenya territory followed until 1967, when agreement was reached with Somalia. Until then most of the Kenyan army had had to be stationed in the north.

Economic achievements and aims. Although the three East African countries are amongst the poorest in the world their industrial activity since independence has been impressive. During the period 1963-6 the annual growth rate of Kenya was 7.5 per cent; of Uganda 10.3 per cent and of Tanganyika 9.6 per cent; an established industrial country like Great Britain had difficulty in maintaining a 3 per cent rate of growth during the same period. Growth in Kenya was assisted by an enlightened policy of conciliation, which resulted in a heavy fall in the number of strikes.

The K.A.N.U. election manifesto of November 1969 emphasised that 'priority will continue to be given to rural development', and a similar stress has been placed on this by both Tanzania and Uganda. East Africa has also proved itself an area of great tourist expansion. Since 1964 the number of visitors to Kenya has increased by 20 per cent every year and tourism now earns a gross national income of about £15 million in foreign currency. In Tanzania construction of a big new airport between Moshi and Arusha was influenced by tourist traffic, as was the increasing construction of new hotels. In Uganda the number of overseas visitors has risen from 8,300 in 1961 to 53,960 in 1968. All three countries have relied on progressive planning. In Uganda in 1968, Dr Obote issued the 'Common Man's Charter', which pointed out that the policy of his party was 'that the resources of the country material and human be exploited for the benefit of all people of Uganda in accordance with the principles of socialism'. Both Kenya and Tanzania have issued government papers outlining a policy of African socialism, and a summary is given in *African Socialism and its Application to Planning in Kenya*, issued by the government of Kenya. It involves 'mutual social responsibility' and 'a range of controls to ensure that property is used in the mutual interests of society and its members'. It was also made clear that the government aimed at increasing the African share of commerce and trade, and so avoiding the inequality that existed when those powerful sections were largely directed by Europeans and Asians.

> Foreign investors should therefore be prepared to accept the spirit of social responsibility, for example –
> (i) by making shares in the company available to Africans who wish to buy them;
> (ii) by employing Africans at managerial levels as soon as qualified people can be found; and
> (iii) by providing training facilities for Africans.

In Tanzania the emphasis has been more on establishing equality between African and African. In *Ujamaa – The Basis of African Socialism*, Dr Nyerere pointed out that in traditional African society, 'Nobody starved, either of food or of human dignity because he lacked personal wealth; he could depend on the wealth possessed by the community of which he was a member. That is socialism.' The relevance of this to a modern African state is shown in the T.A.N.U. creed which was published as part of the Arusha Declaration in 1967. The creed states, 'That it is the responsibility of the State to intervene in the economic life of the Nation so as to ensure the well-being of all citizens and so as to prevent the exploitation of one person by another, or one group by another, and so as to prevent the accumulation of wealth to an extent which is inconsistent with the existence of a classless society.' In setting out the policy of socialism it was also declared that 'The way to build and maintain socialism is to ensure that the major means of production are under the control and ownership of the Peasants and the Workers themselves.'

Finally the creation of the East African community or common market, described in the previous chapter, is an important achievement. Neighbouring states have applied for membership, and if this is granted it could be the basis on which a much larger economic organisation is built.

Africanisation. In Kenya work-permits have been the chief means used to ensure that preference in employment is given to Kenya citizens of all races; by this method the government has avoided identifying class with race. It is in commerce and trade that most wealthy men are found, and before independence most of them were Asians or Europeans. In order that all citizens should share in the rewards of commerce and trade, and to provide opportunities in the professions, the government practice has been to give fewer work-permits than were needed for fully effective working. Pressure was thus put on private concerns to train Africans for responsible jobs. In the public service this policy had been successful throughout East Africa. In Kenya the change was very marked. Before independence only one senior post in seven was held by an African, and most of those in the middle grades were Asian; by 1967 more than half the senior ranks had been Africanised, and about three-quarters of the executive and technical, or middle, grades. Businesses, and in particular the retail-trade, presented a more difficult problem. Much of this employment was in the hands of Asian families, and outsiders could not easily be introduced by work-permits because the concern depended on most of the work being done by members of one family. Moreover, many Asians had believed the British government when it stated that, if on independence they chose British citizenship, they would be able to claim their right to come to England. They had, therefore, not taken out Kenya citizenship within the five years allowed from the declaration of independence. In 1967 a new law on work-permits, which abolished the old category of 'ordinarily resident in Kenya', was passed; henceforth work-permits were required for all except Kenya citizens. They then found themselves excluded from England by new legislation passed there and were too late to secure the right to work in Kenya as Kenyan citizens. This placed them in a very difficult position.

In Uganda since the new trade-licensing laws came into force in December 1969, all Asians who are not citizens have had to close their shops and give their goods away; moreover work-permits for non-citizens are now never extended beyond eight years. As stated by the permanent secretary to the ministry of commerce and industry, Mr Katagyira, 'The purpose of the Trade Licensing Act and the Immigration Control Act is to put more citizens into industry and business.' He went on to add that 'for them to succeed more and more Ugandans must be trained in managerial practices, basic principals of salesmanship, budgeting and simple accounts.' In Tanzania the importance of work was stressed by Dr Nyerere in *Ujamaa – The Basis of African Socialism,* and he gave T.A.N.U. its motto of *Uhuru Na Kazi* or Freedom and Work. A substantial proportion of the population in Tanzania has been involved in self-help, which has been a means of binding the nation together. While efforts are made to avoid racial discrimination, increasing state intervention has inevitably pressed hard on the 135,000 people of Asian origin living in Tanzania in 1968. (While most of them are Tanzanian citizens, from 15,000 to 20,000 hold British 'D' passports.) These are the people who were most affected by the takeover in 1970 of import and wholesale businesses by the State Trading Corporation.

In 1970 social segregation on racial lines had largely disappeared. There was integration now in the schools, hospitals, hotels, buses and railways.

Another pattern of democracy. In *Facing Mount Kenya* Kenyatta pointed out that 'The Gikuyu system of government prior to the advent of the Europeans was based on true democratic principles.' That these principles can be effective in a one-party state has been shown by recent elections in Tanzania and Kenya. In the 1970 election in Kenya, for instance, three cabinet ministers lost their seats to other members of the same party, and in some areas all the sitting members were voted out.

Constitutional changes: Kenya. In December 1964 Kenya became a republic with a national assembly consisting of two houses – the senate and the house of representatives. As the leader of the largest party in the house of representatives, Mzee Jomo Kenyatta, who had been prime minister, became president and head of state, with an executive cabinet of ministers appointed by the president from amongst the members of parliament, and responsible to them. The fundamental rights and freedom of the individual, together with the independence of the judiciary, continued to be guaranteed in the new constitution. Sweeping changes were, however, made in local government. Under the 1963 constitution this was in the hands of seven regional assemblies. In addition the municipal council controlling the Nairobi area was specifically stated to be the city council of Nairobi, and its area was defined. At the time when the constitution was drafted, the smaller tribes, many of whose members supported the K.A.D.U., had stressed the need for a strong local government to protect their interests. It became clear, however, that if Kenya was to develop as a strong unitary state these internal barriers must be abolished, and in August 1964, Mzee Jomo Kenyatta announced that

> The Regional Assemblies are to have no exclusive executive authority or legislative competence in any matter which should be planned and directed on a national scale, for example, education, agriculture, health, economic and social development and the utilization of land ... Regional Assemblies are elected by the districts and those who live in an area may vote for members of the local councils. Councils are expected to levy rates, but the central government will decide on the amount and on what services the local government authorities should provide.

Simultaneously the members of K.A.D.U., headed by their leader, Mr Ngala, crossed the floor, and Kenya became a one-party state until the formation of a new party, the Kenya People's Union (K.P.U.) in 1956, by Oginga Odinga, who claimed that 'A radical change in land policy is obviously necessary ... The K.P.U. is fully committed to secure this change, to correct the highly unjust and inequitable present distribution of land.' Odinga is considered to have had close links with China and has written that 'We are struggling to prevent Kenya's black skins from ruling as successors to the administrators of colonial days.' In 1969 the party had six seats in the representative council but was banned before the next general election. This was postponed till 1970 as part of an arrangement come to with members of the senate, who agreed, on terms, to the senate being merged with the house of representatives to form a national assembly. This incidentally still works to much the same time-table as in more leisurely colonial days. Other problems remain: shortage of land and housing; unemployment, which contributes to juvenile delinquency in Nairobi; competing tribal and national loyalties. Since independence Kenya has made giant strides towards becoming a unified nation, whose stability attracts the capital which can finance further development. The murder of the gifted Tom Mboya, secretary general of K.A.N.U., and minister of economic planning, in 1969, was a shock which was met by a mature country.

Tanganyika becomes a republic. In the final stages before independence it had been all too easy to lose sight of the problems that would come too. Those who believed that independence meant a new prosperity for all Tanganyika citizens found that hospitals and schools took time and money to build, nor could jobs be found for all those who sought them in the towns, and the number of unemployed rose. At the same time the fact that the income per head of the African population was still only about £18, while that of Europeans was many times larger, was naturally resented. In these circumstances the T.A.N.U. left-wing criticised Mwalimu Nyerere's moderate policies, while Europeans, made anxious by four cases of summary deportation, were reluctant to invest in the country; and forty per cent of the expatriates left. Nyerere's offer to resign as prime minister was accepted, and he devoted himself to re-organising the party. In the countryside he stressed the need to revive the traditional policy of self-help.

Tanganyika became a republic on the anniversary of independence, and Mwalimu Nyerere's influence was now so strong in the country that he was able to propose a new constitution based on four principles. These were: a republican government; the rule of law; elected representatives who alone could make laws, raise taxes and vote money; and a president who would be head of state and commander-in-chief of the armed forces, and have full executive authority – he would not even have to accept the advice of his cabinet. In December 1962 Mwalimu Nyerere became President. Soon after this he announced that 'Inasmuch as the people of Tanganyika recognize only one party, the laws of the country must recognize only one party.'

Tanganyika becomes Tanzania. In Africa south of the Sahara only the Union of South Africa had a larger alien élite than the declining Arab aristocracy, to whom control of the island passed when it became independent in December 1963. The way in which their grip on Zanzibar and Pemba was secured has already been described. Many Africans found it hard to understand how their party could cast a majority of votes and yet lose the 1963 election. It looked as though force was the only way of overthrowing the Zanzibar National Party and Pemba People's Party coalition, and the desire to overthrow it was strengthened by such activities as putting party supporters into key jobs and trying to make party loyalty a condition for police membership. Babu, who was the leader of Umma, or the 'party of the masses', was meanwhile stirring up the opposition to substitute Marxist values for those of Islam. Members of his party were found leading all the militant opposition groups. Inadequate precautions against trouble were taken, and in January 1964, a month after the final election, there was a revolution in which a key part was played by a strange character, Okello, who might almost be described as a 'stage revolutionary'. The sultan and his government were driven out. Many lives were lost, and ships sailed from the island tightly packed with deported Arabs. Okello appointed a revolutionary council on which members of Umma were prominent, but after a short interlude Zanzibar was proclaimed a republic with Sheikh Abeid Karume, leader of the Afro-Shirazi Party, as the new president,

Fig. 9   Mwalimu J. K. Nyerere sets an example of self-help

Babu becoming minister for defence and external affairs. This régime, too, was short-lived and the islands of Zanzibar and Pemba are now part of the United Republic of Tanganyika and Zanzibar, which is known as Tanzania. The island is governed by a revolutionary council of thirty which has entire responsibility for its affairs except for external matters and defence. After the revolution a number of Zanzibari came to the mainland, but it is now illegal to do so. Censorship is strict but it is generally accepted that East Germany and China help with capital works and some skilled personnel. It is widely felt that Tanganyika exercises a moderating influence on the island's policy. There is a cabinet of both nations in which Karume holds the office of vice-president; but Zanzibar did not take part in the 1965 or 1970 elections; instead members of the revolutionary council, who belong to the Afro-Shirazi party, became members of the Tanzanian National Association. Zanzibar has declared its opposition to all forms of capitalism.

Tanganyika's social and economic policy. This is set out in the Arusha Declaration and T.A.N.U.'s policy on socialism and self-reliance, to which brief reference was made on pages 196 and 197. Mwalimu Nyerere felt strongly that dependence on foreign governments' companies for help in development meant giving up a part of Tanzania's freedom to act as she chose. In his opinion the real basis for development is the country's fertile and well-watered land and the chief requirement for this development is hard work and intelligence. 'In the villages the women work very hard. At times they work for 12 to 14 hours a day. They even work on Sundays and public holidays . . . but the men who live in villages (and some of the women in towns) are on leave for half of their lives.' Work on the land is therefore required of all those who have been given the privilege of education by the efforts of the country and forms part of the school day, when it is not dodged.

In this austere existence civil servants and political leaders have also to make sacrifices, and not live on a scale far above that of the majority of the people. In 1962, therefore, there were cuts in the pay of senior civil servants and in 1966 there were further cuts from three to twenty per cent in their salaries and in those of political leaders.

Only time will tell whether this unique brand of idealism will succeed in raising Tanzania's standard of living and ensure a stable, progressive government. In external relations Tanzania has moved closer to Zambia lately, and is prepared to accept Chinese help in financing the Zamtan railway, which the western powers were not prepared to support. They may have been influenced in this attitude by Tanzania's determination to extend the scope of public ownership, to which reference was made on page 196. Steps were taken to implement this when all commercial banks, except the Co-operative Bank, all insurance companies and a number of firms were nationalised, and the government took a controlling share in others. Fair compensation was promised, but East Africa is seriously deficient in African qualified chartered accountants, and the amount required for 'fair' compensation exceeded expectations.

Problems facing Uganda on independence. In October 1962, when Uganda became independent, the major problem her prime minister, Dr Milton Obote, faced was neither the assimilation of an alien minority or the gnawing poverty of Tanganyika – it was the overthrow of the feudal régime which still persisted in Buganda. Lesser problems were the lost counties and the position of the Asian traders.

The feudal tradition. In the latter part of the sixteenth century we get the first names in the Buganda list of kings, which included Kintu, who is said to have entered with his people from the Mount Elgon area and eventually to have disappeared with his companion, Nambi, the mother of the race, because he was so distressed at the behaviour of his people. Kintu is a legendary figure, and may well have been the name of a period, but the long line of kabakas was real enough; and Kampala before independence was reminiscent of Versailles before the revolution. Successor to a long line of Buganda kings, Sir Edward Mutesa, kabaka of Buganda, was elected the first president of Uganda, Sir Wilberforce Nadiope, the kyabazinga of Busugo, being the vice-president, but the British queen was still vaguely regarded as the head of state. And the Buganda lukiko resolutely refused to nominate members to the protectorate legislative council (which it feared would become too powerful if supported) until after the 1962 elections, when indirect elections were agreed to. These elections were won by the Uganda People's Congress supported by the Kabaka Yekka (the kabaka's party). The U.P.C. leader, Dr Milton Obote, was therefore appointed prime minister. A year later, in October 1963, Uganda's constitutional position altered when the governor-general was replaced as head of state by a president, elected by the national assembly. The kabaka, by election, became the first president, and Uganda remained in the Commonwealth as an independent sovereign state.

The strain imposed on the constitution by the isolationist attitude of Buganda's feudal hierarchy was considerable, and it was significant that Dr Obote's party was gaining recruits from the Kabaka Yekka party, which looked to the kabaka alone. In January 1966, the appointment of a committee of inquiry, as the result of a motion in the national assembly to investigate the financial activities of the prime ministers and other leading ministers was a danger-signal. Before the committee met Dr Obote had ordered the arrest of five of his ministers and suspended the constitution. Under the new constitution Dr Obote became president and the wings of the kabaka and the Baganda were clipped. The lukiko, however, was not to be daunted and passed a resolution which practically excluded the protectorate government from Buganda. This brought an immediate response: early in the morning of 24 May the protectorate troops captured the kabaka's palace. Sir Edward Mutesa escaped with a few others, and died in England in 1969, but reports speak of a scene of slaughter. In 1971, Dr Obote himself fell from power, as a result of a coup, and was replaced by General Amin.

The affair of the lost counties was settled by a referendum in which the people of Bugangazzi and Buyaga voted to rejoin Bunyoro. This did not meet with entire satisfaction, as Bunyoro claimed more than these two counties.

In 1969 Asiatic shops belonging to Ugandan citizens were still open in Kampala, and the violence of the movement against them has died down, but the Indian control of cotton ginneries has been checked.

Literature. Literature reflects the values of society and the problems of a changing life, and East Africa is now producing some interesting writing. Part of it is autobiographical. In *Child of Two Worlds,* for instance, Mugo Gatheru tells what it means to be a Kikuyu, a Kenyan and an African in the complicated modern world. The son of a medicine man and a member of the 1940 circumcision group, he points out that age-grades 'were like a network or web. In addition the Kikuyu language itself was like a written record. It was built up in a network of numerous proverbs, legends, riddles and fables that were easily transmittable from generation to generation, as in early English society, and in some parts of Europe today.' Later he trained at the medical research laboratory in Nairobi as a technician, before editing *The Africa Voice* for K.A.N.U. Finally he went to India, and so to the United States, where as a post-graduate student in psychology he was interested 'to find the extent of the problem of maladjustment in the industrial society of the white man', and comments that 'Problems of maladjustment occur almost as frequently in a so-called simple, agricultural community like Kikuyuland.' They are particularly acute where husband and wife hold different values, as the lament by Okot P. Bitek, called *Song of Lawino,* shows. Ocol is married to an uneducated wife who does not know:

How many days
>> There are in a year
>> And how many weeks
>> In four months.

Yet he insists on the exact time when

>> He should have morning tea and breakfast,
>> When exactly to have coffee
>> And the exact time
>> For taking the family photograph.

He wants her to use a primus stove, but she does not know how to light it.

>> And when it gets blacked
>> How can I prick it?
>> The thing roars
>> Like a male lion.

'I am not', she says, 'a shy woman', and she does not hesitate to ask intelligent questions, for she does not despise the ways of foreigners, but does find it difficult to understand them. Bitek's satire draws attention to the problems she and her half-educated husband face in choosing what is worth having in the new ways without losing sight of traditional and different ways of life.

James Ngugi is another promising writer, specialising in fiction; in 1964 he won the first prize at Dakar Festival of Negro Arts for his novel, *Weep Not Child,* which describes the effect of Mau-Mau on life in a Kenyan village and on the love-affair of two youngsters who grew up under its shadow. It makes a very readable book, but as a child is the hero, the description of events is obviously limited. In *The River Between,* which he published next, Ngugi concentrates on the conflict within society which is symbolised by Kameno and Mukuyu. His third novel, *A Grain of Wheat,* takes the same period of time, but by now his skill as a writer had developed to the point where he was able to describe the village of Thabai and its inhabitants with such understanding that the reader is introduced to a new world. Already Ngugi is a leading novelist whose gift of expression is to be envied.

Potent Ash, a collection of short stories by Leonard Kibera and Samuel Kahiga, also deals with Kenya's terrible Emergency, and shows that writers are now sufficiently remote from events to be able to sketch home guards and freedom fighters as real people, not puppets. In 'Departure at Dawn', for instance, convincing dialogue and description show the strain on a Kikuyu family who sheltered a wounded freedom fighter in their hut on a European farm. At first Mugo's schoolboy son is fascinated by his uncle's adventurous life, but later he is disturbed by the risks his own father is taking in letting him stay.

'Don't you know that our ancestors' eyes follow us everywhere? You break the law today, or tomorrow, their eyes can see you', remarks a character in Grace Ogot's novel, *The Promised Land,* which is about Luo pioneers in Tanzania; yet she herself is a pioneer in the new life East African women lead. Trained as a nurse, she has been a script-writer and a community development officer as well as a public relations officer for an airline, and now runs her own business.

Art. In Chapter 1 reference was made to the early rock paintings found in caves. Descendants of these gifted artists may well be among the Makerere students who decorated the Mary Stuart hall of residence at the university with lively frescoes. But for the most part the indigenous art in East Africa was confined to designs for weaving, basketry, the decoration of calabashes and pottery, which flourished in villages, and were largely ignored by Europeans in the early years of the twentieth century. In their own country the English recognised that art had a place in the education of designers and professional people, but as these were not looked for in Africans art education was not considered to be a necessary part of African education. As a leading art critic commented, in 1929 in *Overseas Education,* 'In our colonial and imperial responsibilities we failed too often to value the active culture which shows its presence through creative power.' On the coast this 'active culture' took the form of metal-working; mosaic patterns of leather mats also have been found in the Lamu area. Inland the Maasai also boast well-decorated leather shields, and their womenfolk have fine leather coats. If the loom had existed in East Africa there would have been an obvious link with western craftsmanship, but as it was, the village craftsman was ignored by European educationists and administrators and despised by his fellows, who were educated and lived in urban surroundings. Today the Kamba craftsmen sell their wares in New York, but even nine years ago a skilled carver of wood was described to the author as a failure who had no hope of a secondary education.

In 1937 Mrs Trowell started the Makerere art department, in which teaching was based not on European models but on traditional forms, which suggested the rhythm and movement behind successful design. This was the beginning of an East African renaissance in art, a forum for which was provided by the Pas-ya-Paa Gallery in Nairobi, whose director, Elimo Njau, created the impressive frescoes in the church at Fort Hall, which commemorate the suffering endured in the Mau-Mau rising.

Fig. 10   An example of Makonde sculpture

Recently considerable interest has been attracted by a group of Makonde artists, who live in a remote part of Tanzania. In their 1969 exhibition of wood sculpture at the Grosvenor galleries in London they showed an apparently endless capacity to present a vital sensuous spirit world. The influence of African artists, particularly those of West Africa, on artists at the beginning of the twentieth century is well known, and in this exhibition it was interesting to note the resemblance between the work of that great artist Picasso in his 1920 period and that of the Makonde sculptors of today.

Music. An African schoolboy wrote in the records of the Kamusinga History Society, 'If I had the ability I would try to research into African music, because I discovered that most of the stories of the past are still told in the form of music.' There are songs also for all the rites of nature and man; a collection of these would further enrich the records of African life in the past. These songs vary from group to group, for music is based primarily on the sound of the vernacular. *Uro, uro, oe',* for example, a milking-song of the Kipsigis, will not be heard on the coast where the Islamic musical tradition has widely penetrated.

The serious study of African music is, however, handicapped by the lack of reliable scores; these are needed before it can be appreciated by the world's musicians. In East Africa, where the music can be heard it is already valued highly; the Embu drummers, for instance, can draw an audience many politicians would envy. Their performance illustrates one of the difficulties which have held up the writing of scores; in drumming they are playing tunes, and the score needs to show the tune as well as the rhythm. This makes it much more complicated to write down. Another difficulty lies in the spontaneous variations often introduced by master drummers; a practice we are familiar with in jazz.

In *Facing Mount Kenya* Kenyatta draws attention to an interesting aspect of the function of musical instruments among the Kikuyu: the sex of the musicians and the nature of the occasions decide which instrument is to be used. After pointing out that the majority of Kikuyu dances and songs are performed without any musical instruments, he goes on to describe the four Kikuyu musical instruments and their function in society. The most prominent is the flute: 'There is no cut-and-dried rule as to how a flute may be made or played. The technique depends entirely on the individual's taste. Some people prefer four holes, others six or eight holes. The materials also differ.' It is usually played with a sense of humour, for enjoyment, or to comfort a man when he is feeling lonely and sometimes to please the women, who traditionally do not play the flute. Next the drum, which among the Kikuyu is 'restricted to a very few ceremonial dances and songs. The use of drums as musical instruments has been adopted only in recent years, the idea was borrowed from the Wakamba.' News used to be sent by the horn but is now, of course, heard over the radio or read in the newspapers, of which there are seven in the English medium, in addition to six, in the vernacular. Finally there are two kinds of rattles used in dances, the Kegamba and the Njingiri. Except for initiation ceremonies the use of the first is restricted to men.

SUGGESTIONS FOR FURTHER READING

The titles given are of books recommended for schools building a reference library.

East African History needs to be reviewed in a wider setting and for this purpose an excellent introduction is *A Short History of Africa,* Oliver & Fage (Penguin). It might be supplemented by *Africa and the Victorians,* R. Robinson and O. Gallagher (Macmillan), which provides an interesting analysis of the motives behind the European involvement in Africa. An *Atlas of African Affairs,* ed. Boyd and Van Rensburg (Methuen, University Paperbacks), provides a geographical background to contemporary events; and *African Mythology,* G. Parrinder (Hamlyn), has over 120 good illustrations of African Art at a price within the range of school libraries. East African writers are available in Heinemann African Writers Series, the East African Publishing House and Penguin Books.

Useful articles on particular aspects of East African History can be found in copies of the *Uganda Journal,* which has a literary issue entitled *Chala* and *Tanganyika Notes & Records.* Then there are the short publications of the Historical Association of Tanzania. These include *The East African Coast,* J. E. G. Sutton (East African Publishing House); *The East African Slave Trade,* E. A. Alpers (E.A.P.H.); and *Records of the Maji Maji Rising* ed. G. C. K. Gwassar and John Iliffe (E.A.P.H.).

Since the output of books on Africa has become a flood, the remaining suggestions are limited to those dealing specifically with East Africa. The following are written at the level of the teacher, rather than the pupil, and some are relatively expensive. *History of East Africa,* Vol. 1 ed. R. Oliver and G. Mathew (available in paperback), Vol. 2 ed. V. Harlow and E. M. Chilver (O.U.P.); *A History of Zanzibar from the Middle Ages to 1856,* Sir John Gray (O.U.P.); *The Origins of European Settlement in Kenya,* M. P. K. Sorrenson (O.U.P.); *Zamani, A Survey of East African History,* ed. B. A. Ogot and J. A. Kieran (E.A.P.H.); *Islam & East Africa,* R. Oliver (Longmans); *Haddith Conference of the Historical Association of Kenya,* ed. B. A. Ogot (International Publication Service).

Extracts from good secondary and primary sources are to be found in *East Africa Through Contemporary Records,* Z. Marsh (C.U.P.); *African Discovery,* M. Perham & J. Simmons (Faber), also provides an excellent anthology of the writings of the explorers.

Other books which pupils, as well as teachers, may like to read are listed below, grouped roughly according to the period they cover.

Prelude to East African History, M. Posnansky (O.U.P.).

Men and Monuments on the East African Coast, J. S. Kirkman (Lutterworth Press).

History of the Chagga People of Kilimanjaro, K. M. Stahl (Mouton).

Facing Mount Kenya, Mzee Jomo Kenyatta (Secker and Warburg).

The Making of Tanganyika, Judith Listowel (Chatto and Windus).

Kenya, A Political History, George Bennett (O.U.P.).

Freedom and Unity, Mwalimu Julius Nyerere (O.U.P.).

A History of Zanzibar 1934–1964, S. G. Ayany

Buganda in Modern History, D. A. Low (C.U.P.).

Form Three pupils, as well as those from Form Four, should enjoy reading the following relatively inexpensive books:-

The Freeing of the Slaves in East Africa, J. J. Mbotela (Evans).

Mutesa of Uganda, Dr Kiwanuka (East African Literature Bureau).

Omukama Chwa II Kabarega, A. R. Dunbar (E.A.L.B.).

Nabongo Mumia, John Osogo (E.A.L.B.).

John Ainsworth, F. H. Goldsmith (E.A.L.B.).

The Story of a Railway, Patrick Pringle Evans (E.A.L.B.).

INDEX

Abajunta people, 13–14
African Association, 49, 89, 90, 91
Africanisation, in Kenya, 175, 177, 197
Afro-Shirazi Party, Zanzibar, 192, 194, 200, 202
agriculture: Kenya, 113–15, 144, 147, 150–1, 171, 172; Tanganyika, 124, 158, 186, 187; Uganda, 144, 152, 154, 179–81; Zanzibar, 70, 87
air services, 165, 173, 196
akidas, 125, 138, 140, 157
Albert, Lake, 55, 58, 137
Albuquerque, A. d', 27
Ali bin al-Hasan, Sultan, 24
Almeida, F. d', 25, 28
Amani research centre, 127
Amin, General, 204
Ankole, 42, 101, 120, 135, 136
Anti-Slavery Society, 107
Arabs: in Central Africa, 42, 54, 57, 73; in East Africa, 17, 18–19, 21–2, 24, 36; and Germans, 126, 131–2, 138; and missions, 82–3; in Zanzibar, Britain and, 132, 141
art, 3, 206–7
Arthington, R., 81
Arthur, Dr, missionary, 149
Arusha, 126; Arusha Declaration (1967), 192, 196, 202

Babu, Zanzibar Marxist, 200, 201
Bagomoyo, 72, 80, 138
Baker, Sir S., 55, 76, 88, 136
bananas, 7–8, 12, 42, 139
Bangwelu, Lake, 58
Bantu peoples, 7, 14–15, 15–16, 20
banyans, 45, 70, 73, 74
Banyole people, 9, 12
Baptist Missionary Society, 78
Barbosa, Duarte, 25
Baring, Sir E., Governor of Kenya, 169
Bechuanaland, 93
Belfield, Sir H., Governor of Kenya, 116
Belgium, 145; *see also* Congo, Belgian
Bell, Sir H., Governor of Uganda, 122
Berlin Conference (1884–5), 92, 131
bicycles, 122, 153
Bigo, Bunyoro centre, 9–10
Bismarck, O. von, 91, 92, 93, 94, 96, 131

Bitek, O. P., writer, 204–5
Bito dynasties, in Uganda, 10, 11, 40–1
Blood, Sir H., 193; Blood Commission, 194
Blundell, Sir M., political leader, Kenya, 175
Brava, 68, 89
Britain: and East Africa, 33, 34; treaties of, with France (1862), 84, with Germany (1886) 96, 97, (1890) 97, 99–100, 102, 141, with Oman (1798), 66, with Portugal (1884), 91, with Seyyid Said (1822), 67, 68, 85, with Zanzibar (1873), 86; and West Africa, 78; *see also* British East Africa, Kenya Colony, Tanganyika, Zanzibar
British Commonwealth, 195
British East Africa Association, 96, 98
British East Africa Protectorate (Kenya), 104, 105, 109–18, 140; Eastern province of Uganda ceded to, 112, 121, 137; renamed Kenya Colony, 143
British and Foreign Bible Society, 78
British India Steam Navigation Company, 34, 87
Bruce, James, explorer, 49
Buddu province, Uganda, 102, 103, 135, 136
Buganda, 10, 36, 41, 42; Britain and, 118–19, 120, 134–6, 137; increasing strength of, 130, 141; missions in, 81–2; and Uganda, 182–4, 203–4
Bukoba, 125, 128, 140, 157
Bulwanyi, battle at (1890), 101
Bunyoro (Kitara) confederation, 9, 10, 40–2, 75; Britain and, 118, 120, 136–7, 141; claimed for Sudan, 88; counties lost by, 209
Burton, Sir R., explorer, 53, 54–5
Bushiri bin Salim, 98, 99, 131, 137, 160
Bushmen, 7
Busoga, 10, 75; Busoga railway, 122, 152
Bwana Heri, 98, 137
Byatt, Sir H., Governor of Tanganyika, 156

Cameron, Sir D., Governor of Tanganyika, 40, 156–7, 163, 189
cannibals, 72
Canning Award (1861), 84